BIG-NOTE PIANO

2ND EDITION

BEST OF
TAYLOR SWIFT

Cover photo © Getty Images / Jun Sato / TAS18 / Contributor

ISBN 978-1-5400-9067-6

Visit Hal Leonard Online at
www.halleonard.com

Contact us:
Hal Leonard
7777 West Bluemound Road
Milwaukee, WI 53213
Email: info@halleonard.com

In Europe, contact:
Hal Leonard Europe Limited
42 Wigmore Street
Marylebone, London, W1U 2RN
Email: info@halleonardeurope.com

In Australia, contact:
Hal Leonard Australia Pty. Ltd.
4 Lentara Court
Cheltenham, Victoria, 3192 Australia
Email: info@halleonard.com.au

BACK TO DECEMBER

Words and Music by
TAYLOR SWIFT

Moderately, in 2

mf

1. I'm so glad you made time to see me. How's life?
2. *(See additional lyrics)*

Tell me, how's your fam - 'ly? I have - n't seen _____ them in _____ a

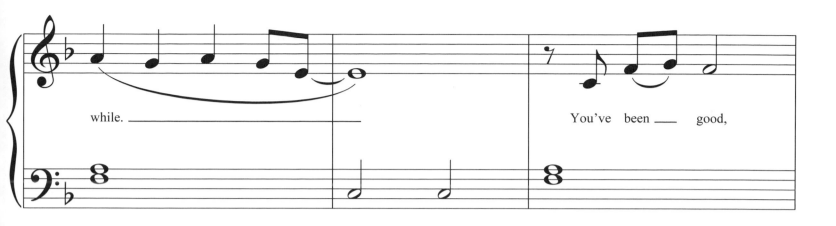

while. _____ You've been ___ good,

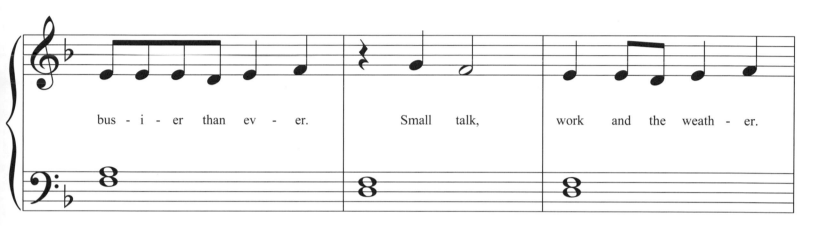

bus - i - er than ev - er. Small talk, work and the weath - er.

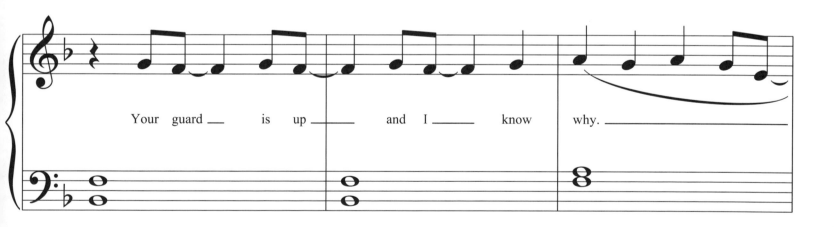

Your guard ___ is up ___ and I ___ know why. _____

___ Be - cause the last time you saw me it still

burned in the back of your mind. You gave me ros - es and I ____

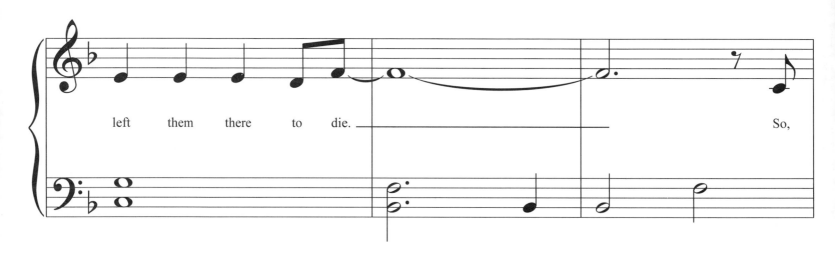

left them there to die. ____ So,

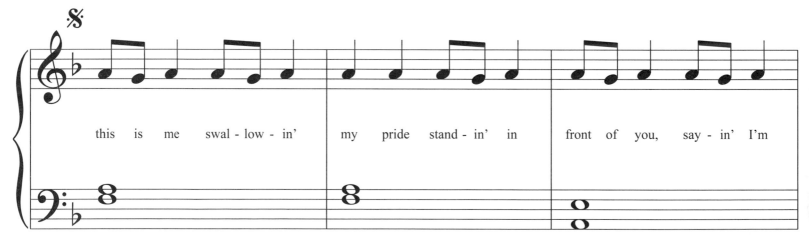

this is me swal - low - in' my pride stand - in' in front of you, say - in' I'm

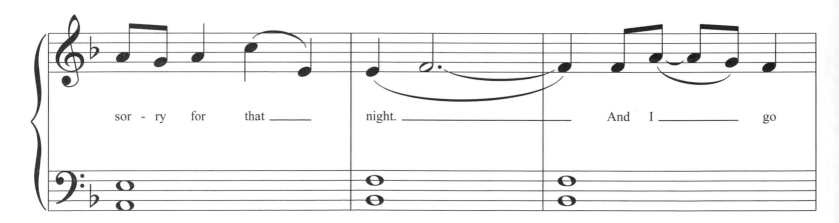

sor - ry for that ____ night. ____ And I ____ go

back to De - cem - ber all _____ the time. ___ It turns out free - dom ain't

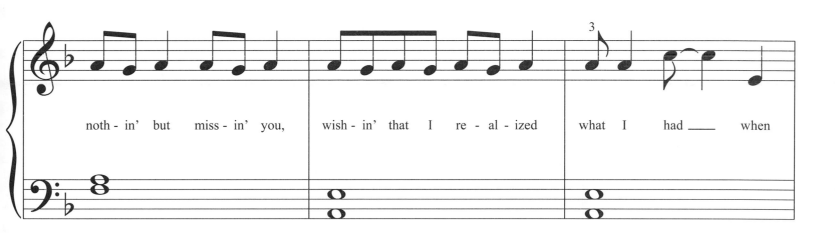

noth - in' but miss - in' you, wish - in' that I re - al - ized what I had ___ when

you were mine. _____ I _____ go back to De - cem - ber,

To Coda

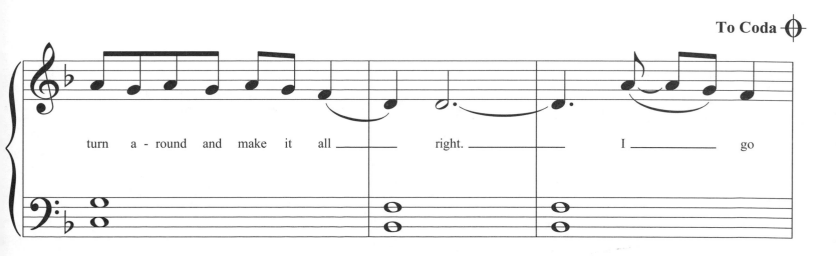

turn a - round and make it all _____ right. _____ I _____ go

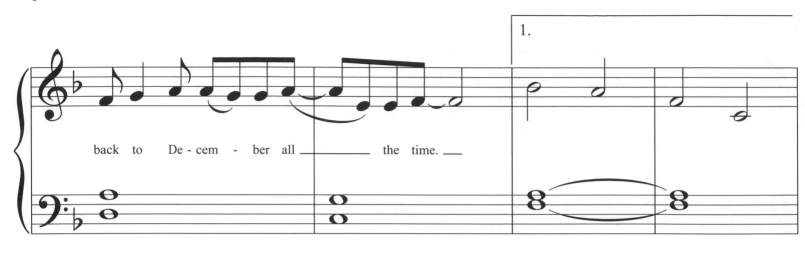

back to De - cem - ber all _____ the time. ___

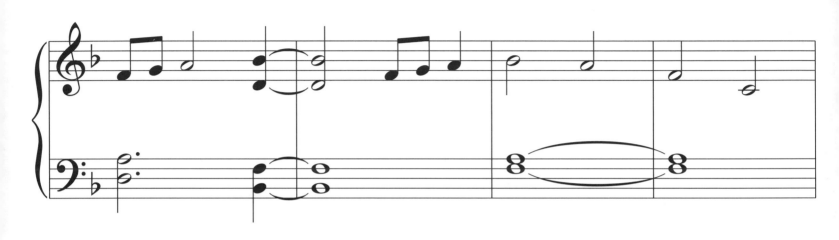

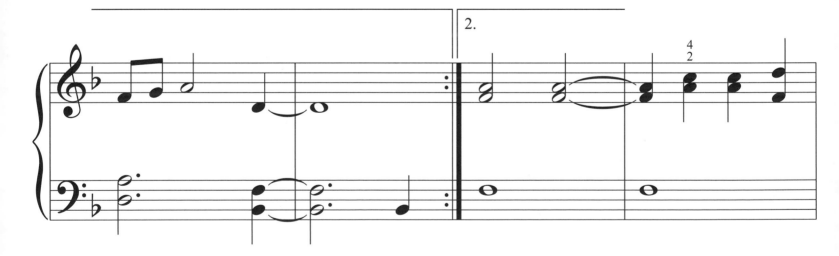

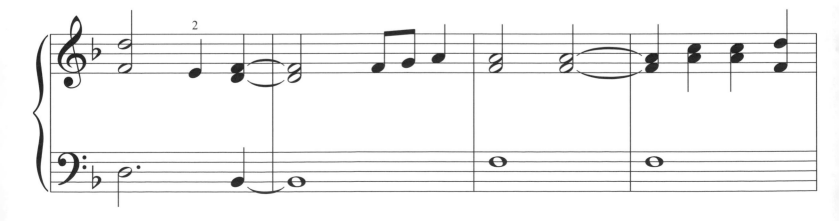

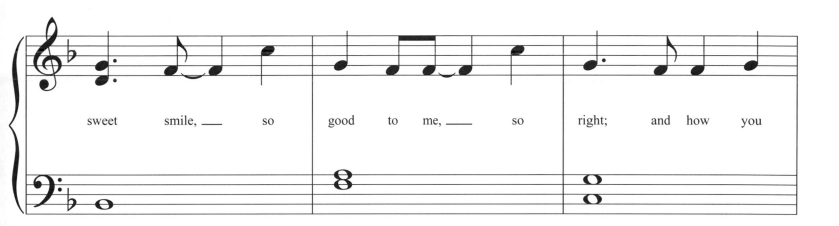

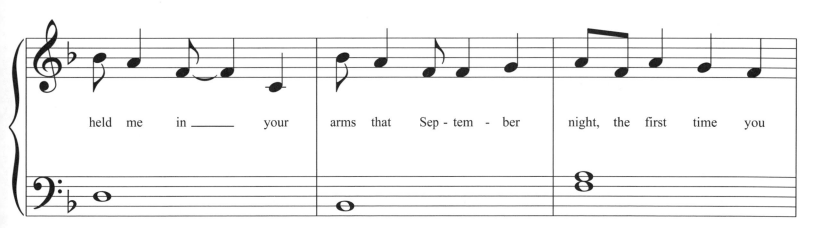

prob - a - bly   mind - less dream - in'.   If we loved a - gain, ___

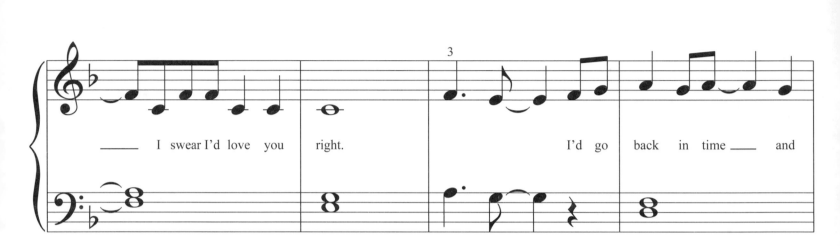

___ I swear I'd love you right.   I'd go back in time ___ and

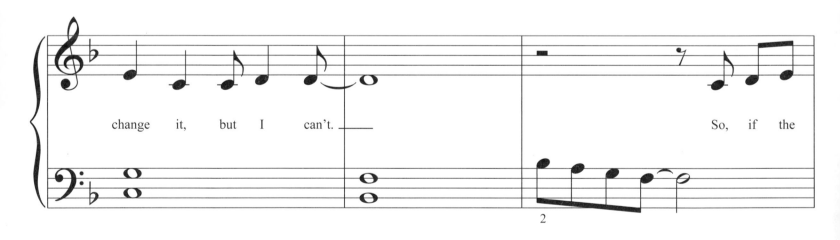

change it, but I can't. ___   So, if the

D.S. al Coda

chain is on ___ your door, I un - der - stand.   But

CODA

back to De - cem - ber all _____ the time. __

poco rit.

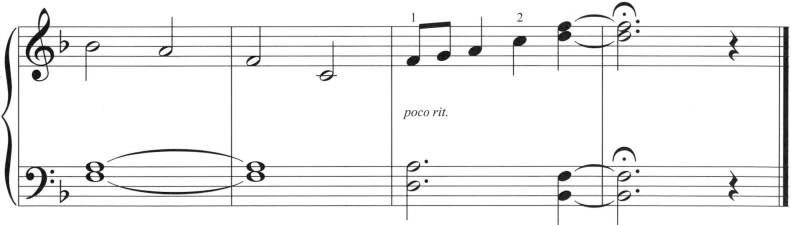

Additional Lyrics

2. These days I haven't been sleepin';
   Stayin' up, playin' back myself leavin',
   When your birthday passed and I didn't call.
   Then I think about summer, all the beautiful times
   I watched you laughin' from the passenger side
   And realized I loved you in the fall.
   And then the cold came, the dark days
   When fear crept into my mind.
   You gave me all your love and
   All I gave you was goodbye.

   So, this is me swallowin' my pride...

LOVE STORY

Words and Music by
TAYLOR SWIFT

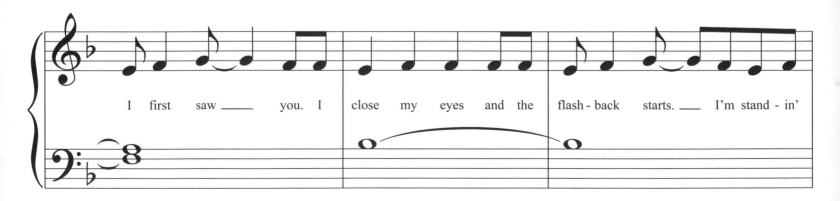

you were Ro - me - o.   You were throw - ing peb - bles, and my
you were Ro - me - o, I was the scar - let let - ter, and my

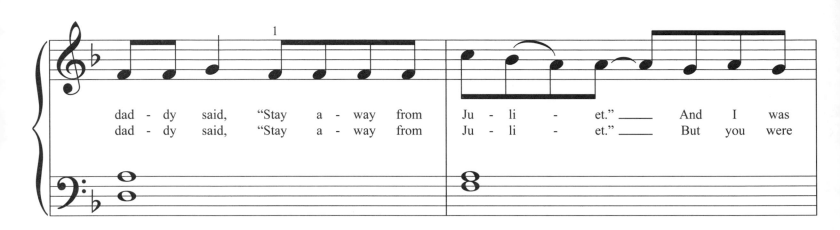

dad - dy said, "Stay a - way from Ju - li - et." ___ And I was
dad - dy said, "Stay a - way from Ju - li - et." ___ But you were

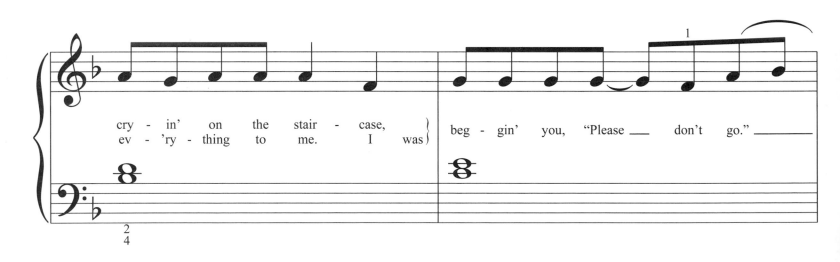

cry - in' on the stair - case,   beg - gin' you, "Please ___ don't go." ___
ev - 'ry - thing to me.   I was

___   And I said, "Ro - me - o, take me

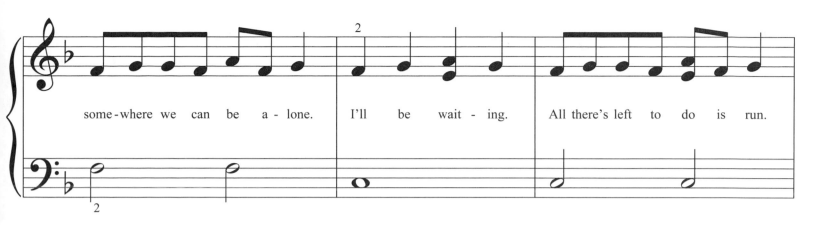

some - where we can be a - lone.   I'll be wait - ing.   All there's left to do is run.

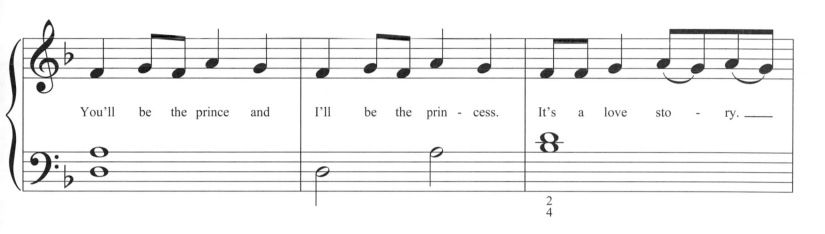

You'll be the prince and   I'll be the prin - cess.   It's a love sto - ry. ____

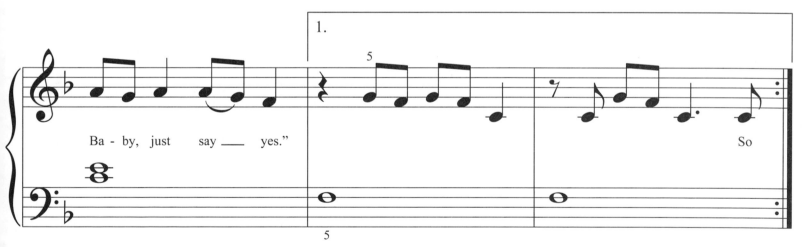

1.

Ba - by, just say ___ yes."   So

2.

"Ro - me - o, save me. They're try'n' to tell me how to feel.   This love is dif - fi - cult,

but it's ___ real. ___ Don't be a - fraid. We'll make it out of this mess.

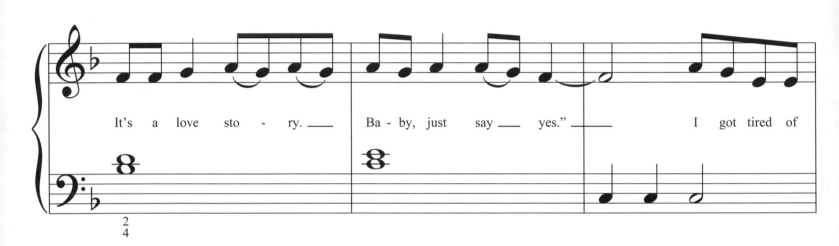

It's a love sto - ry. ___ Ba - by, just say ___ yes." ___ I got tired of

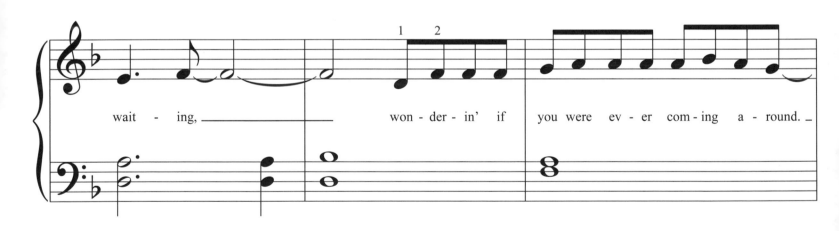

wait - ing, ___ won - der - in' if you were ev - er com - ing a - round. ___

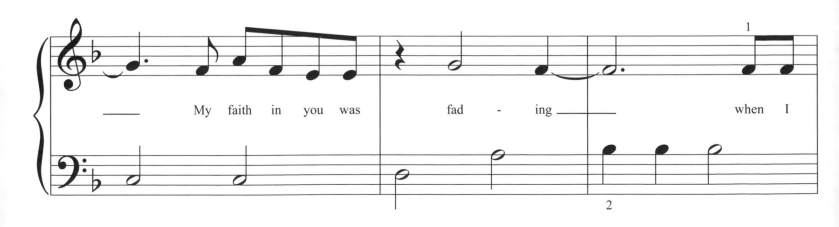

___ My faith in you was fad - ing ___ when I

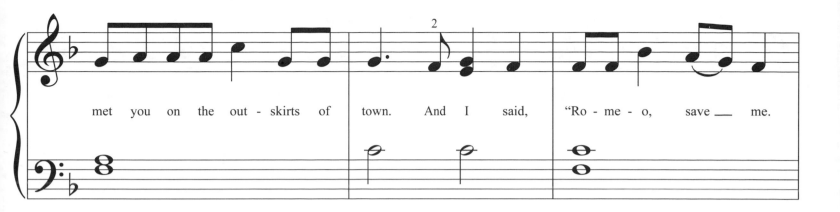

met you on the out - skirts of town. And I said, "Ro - me - o, save ___ me.

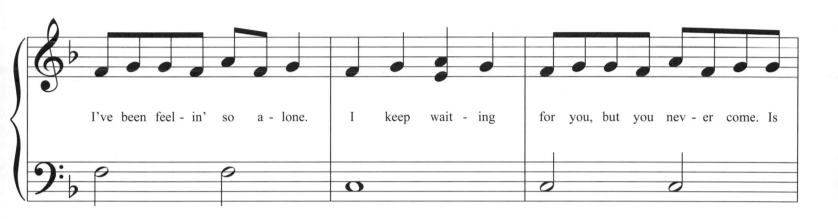

I've been feel - in' so a - lone. I keep wait - ing for you, but you nev - er come. Is

this in my head? I don't know what to think." He knelt to the ground and

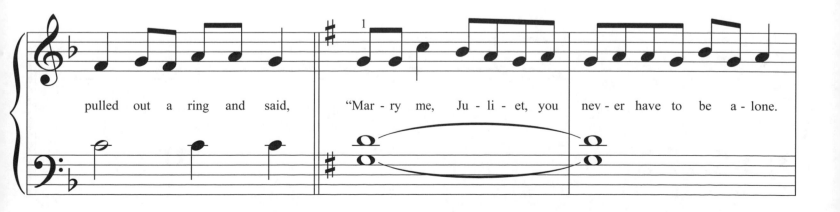

pulled out a ring and said, "Mar - ry me, Ju - li - et, you nev - er have to be a - lone.

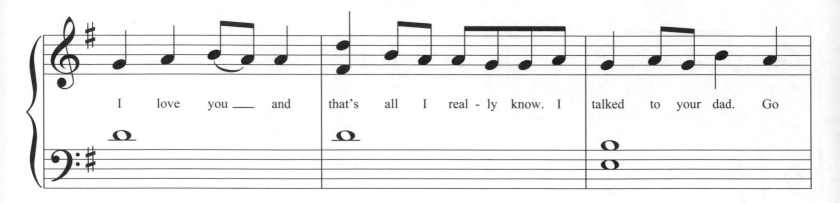

I love you ___ and that's all I real - ly know. I talked to your dad. Go

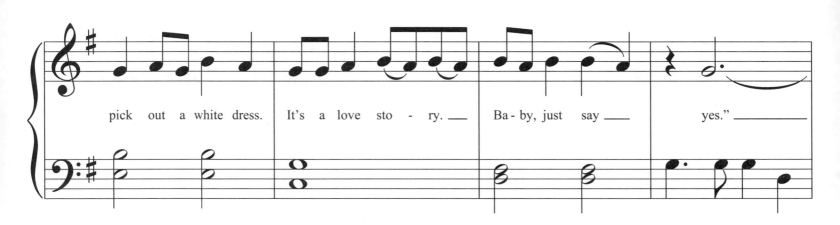

pick out a white dress. It's a love sto - ry. ___ Ba - by, just say ___ yes." ___

___ Oh, oh, oh, ___ oh, oh, oh, oh.

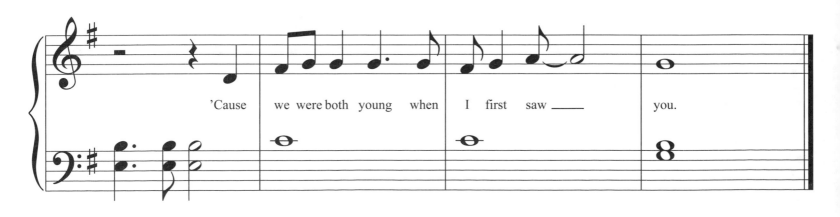

'Cause we were both young when I first saw ___ you.

BLANK SPACE

Words and Music by TAYLOR SWIFT,
MAX MARTIN and SHELLBACK

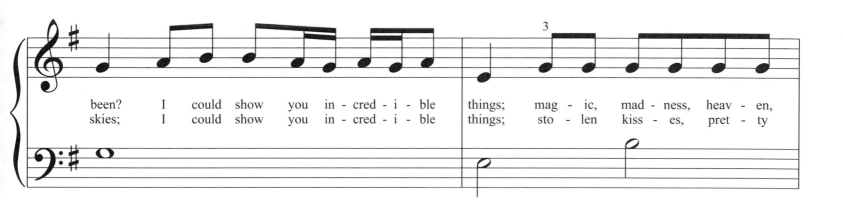

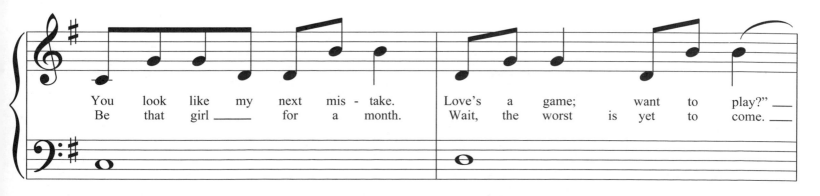

Eh.
Oh, no.

New mon - ey, suit and
Scream - ing, cry - ing, per - fect

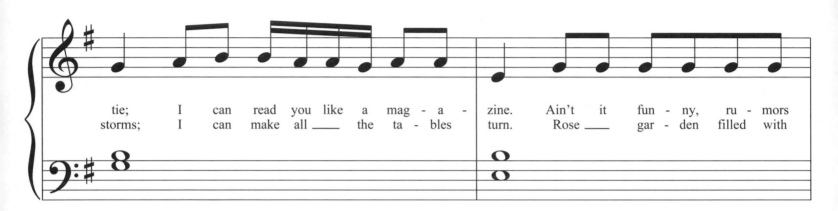

tie; I can read you like a mag - a - zine. Ain't it fun - ny, ru - mors
storms; I can make all ___ the ta - bles turn. Rose ___ gar - den filled with

fly, and I know you heard a - bout me. So hey, let's be friends. I'm
thorns; keep you sec - ond - guess - ing like: "Oh my God, who is she?"

dy - ing to see how this one ends. But
I ___ get drunk on jeal - ous - y. But

Grab your pass - ports and my hand.
you'll come back each time you leave, 'cause

19

'Cause you know I love the play - ers and you love the game.

'Cause we're young and we're reck - less, we'll take this way too far. ___

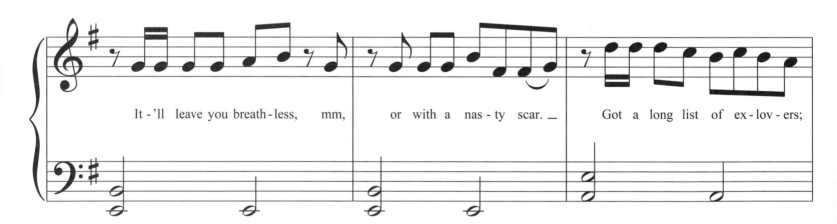

It -'ll leave you breath-less, mm, or with a nas - ty scar. _ Got a long list of ex - lov - ers;

To Coda ⊕

they'll tell you I'm in - sane. But I've got a blank space, ba - by, and I'll write your name.

I KNEW YOU WERE TROUBLE

Words and Music by TAYLOR SWIFT,
SHELLBACK and MAX MARTIN

Moderately fast

Once up-on a time a few mis-takes a-go, I was in your sights,
No a-pol-o-gies, he'll nev-er see you cry. Pre-tends he does-n't know that

you got me a-lone. You found ____ me, you found ____ me, you
he's the rea-son why you're drown - ing, you're drown - ing, you're

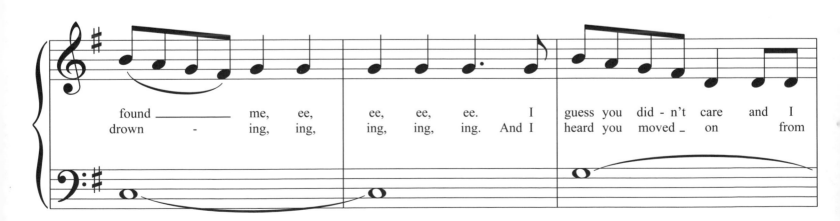

found ____ me, ee, ee, ee, ee. I guess you did-n't care and I
drown - ing, ing, ing, ing, ing. And I heard you moved _ on from

guess I liked that. And when I fell hard, you took a step back with-
whis - pers on the street. A new notch in your belt is all I'll ev - er be. And

out _____ me, with - out _____ me, with - out _____ me, ee,
now _____ I see, now _____ I see, now _____ I see, ee,

ee, ee, ee. _____ And he's long _____
ee, ee, ee. _____ He was long _____

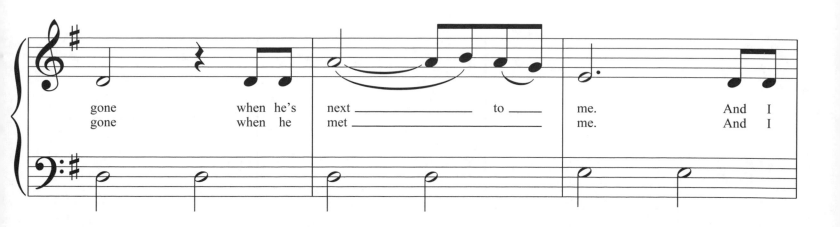

gone when he's next _____ to _____ me. And I
gone when he met _____ me. And I

re - a - lize _____ the blame is on _____ me. _____
re - a - lize _____ the joke is on _____ me. _____ } 'Cause

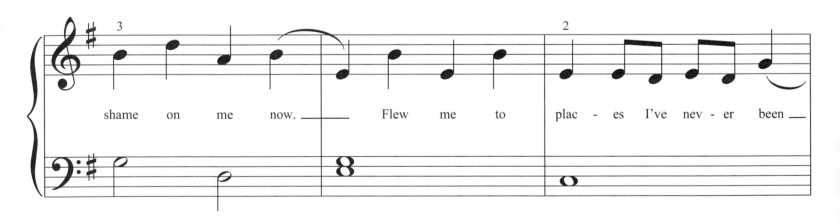

I knew you were trou - ble when you walked in, _____ so

shame on me now. _____ Flew me to plac - es I've nev - er been _____

_____ 'til you put me down. Oh, I knew you were

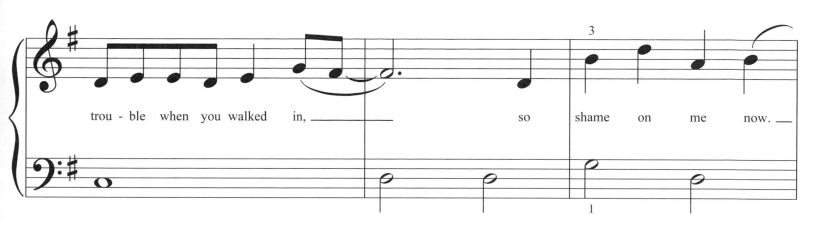

trou - ble when you walked in, _____ so shame on me now. _____

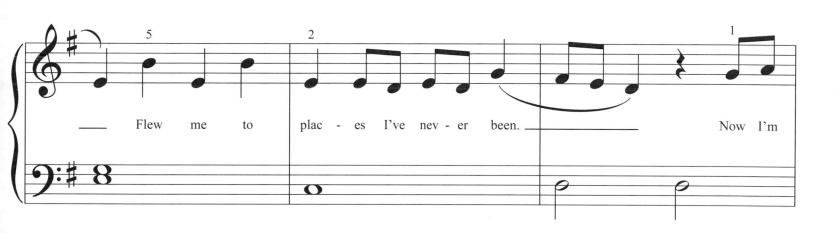

_____ Flew me to plac - es I've nev - er been. _____ Now I'm

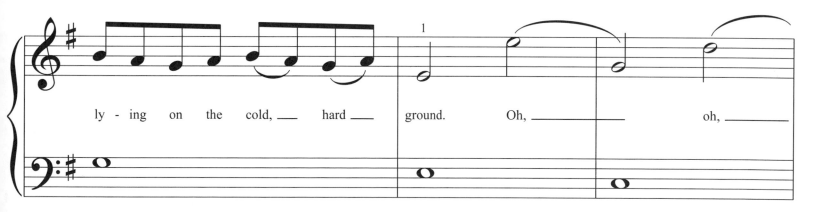

ly - ing on the cold, ___ hard ___ ground. Oh, _____ oh, _____

_____ trou - ble, trou - ble, trou - ble. Oh, _____

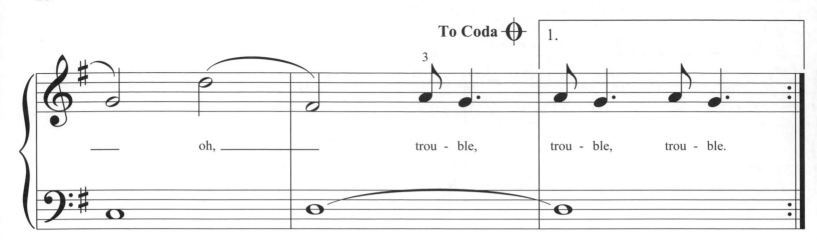

oh, _____ trou - ble, trou - ble, trou - ble.

trou - ble, trou - ble. And the sad - dest fear _____ comes

creep - in' in, _____ that you nev - er loved me

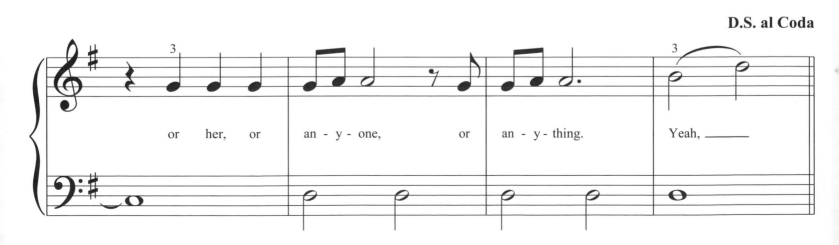

or her, or an - y - one, or an - y - thing. Yeah, _____

CODA

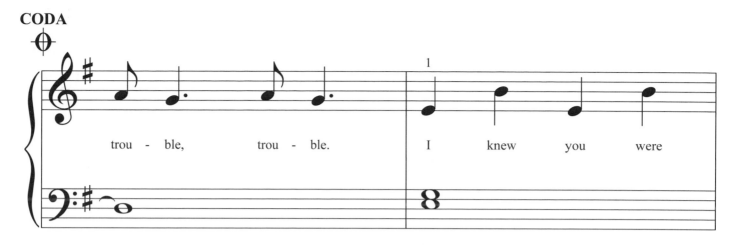

trou - ble,   trou - ble.   I   knew   you   were

trou - ble when you walked   in.   Trou - ble,

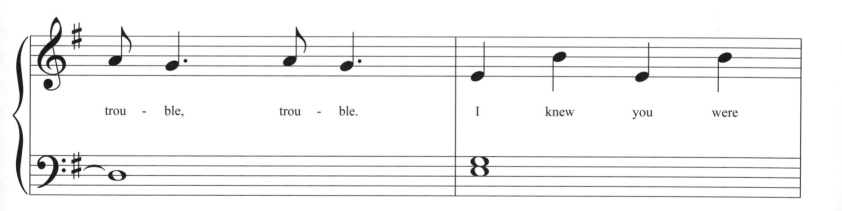

trou - ble,   trou - ble.   I   knew   you   were

trou - ble when you walked   in.   Trou - ble,   trou - ble,   trou - ble.

LOOK WHAT YOU MADE ME DO

Words and Music by TAYLOR SWIFT,
JACK ANTONOFF, RICHARD FAIRBRASS,
FRED FAIRBRASS and ROB MANZOLI

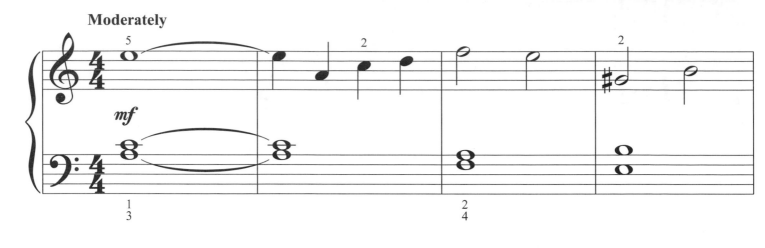

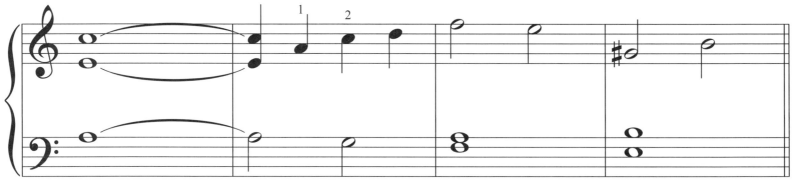

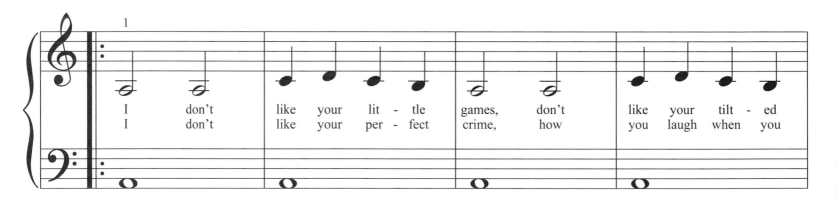

I don't like your lit - tle games, don't like your tilt - ed
I don't like your per - fect crime, how you laugh when you

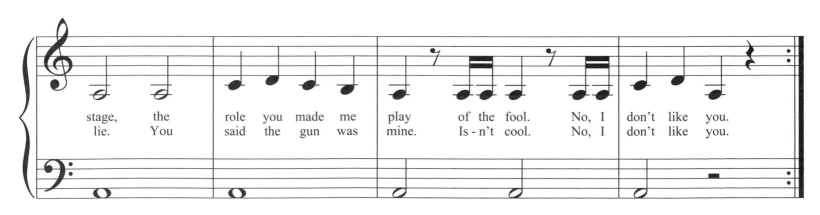

stage, the role you made me play of the fool. No, I don't like you.
lie. You said the gun was mine. Is - n't cool. No, I don't like you.

Ooh, look what you made me do, look what you made me

To Coda ⊕

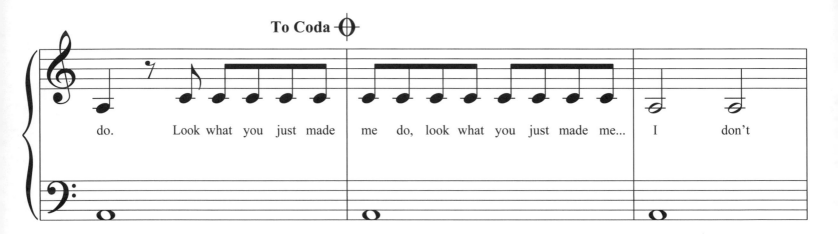

do. Look what you just made me do, look what you just made me... I don't

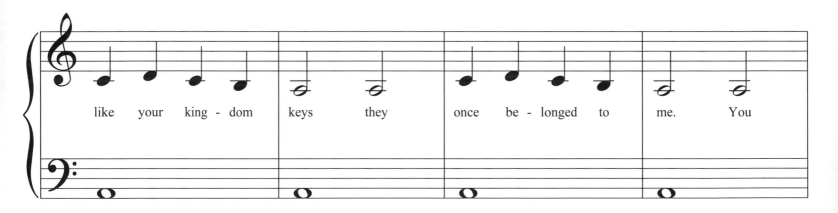

like your king - dom keys they once be - longed to me. You

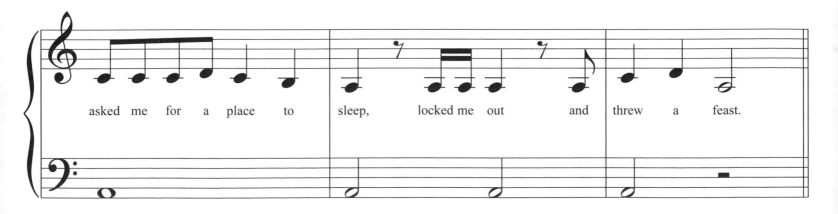

asked me for a place to sleep, locked me out and threw a feast.

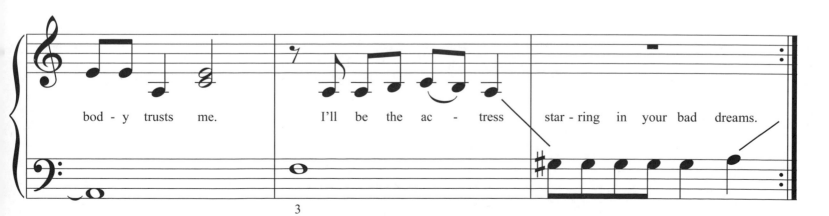

3

I don't trust no-bod-y and no-bod-y trusts me. I'll be the ac - tress

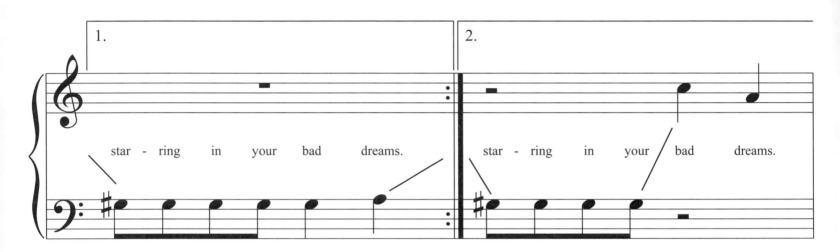

1. star - ring in your bad dreams.

2. star - ring in your bad dreams.

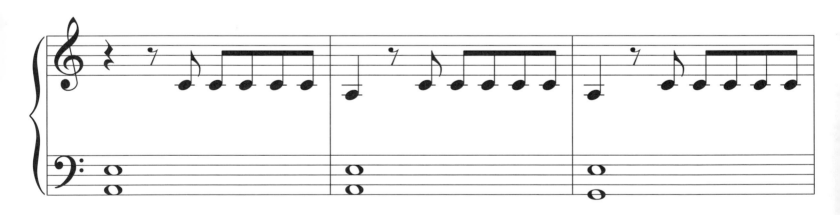

(Spoken:) "I'm sorry, the old Taylor *can't come to the phone right now.* *Why?*

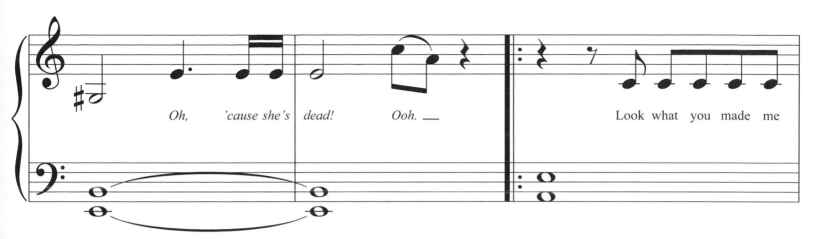

Play 3 times

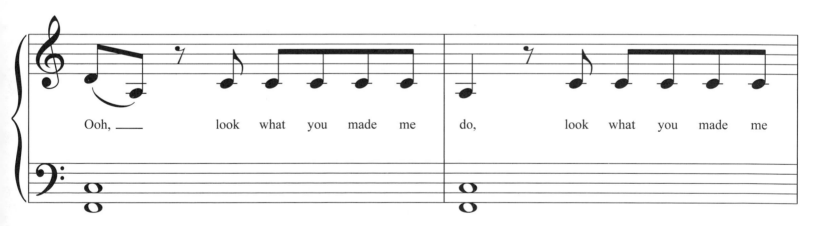

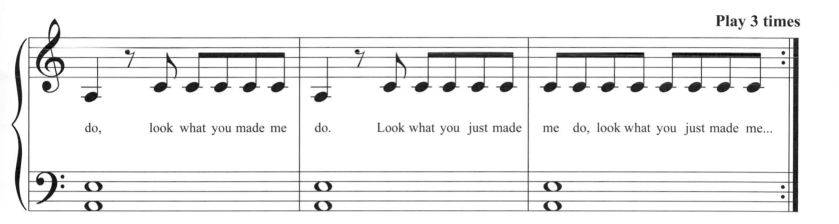

LOVER

Words and Music by
TAYLOR SWIFT

We could leave the Christ-mas lights up 'til Jan-u-ar-y.

This is our place, we make the rules. ___ And there's a

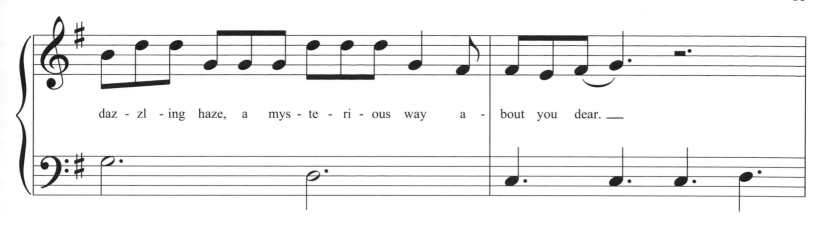

daz - zl - ing haze, a mys - te - ri - ous way a - bout you dear. ___

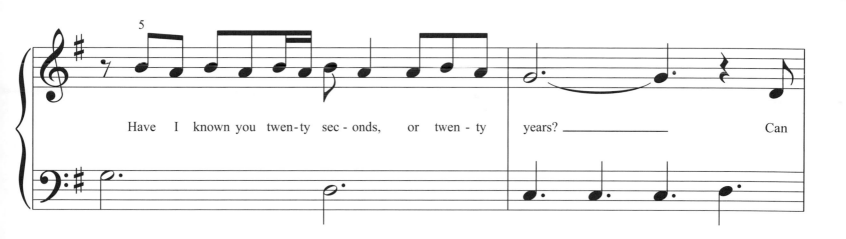

Have I known you twen - ty sec - onds, or twen - ty years? _____ Can

I go where you go? _____ Can we al - ways be this

close? _____ For - ev - er and ev - er, ah, ___ take me out and take me home. _____ You're

To Coda

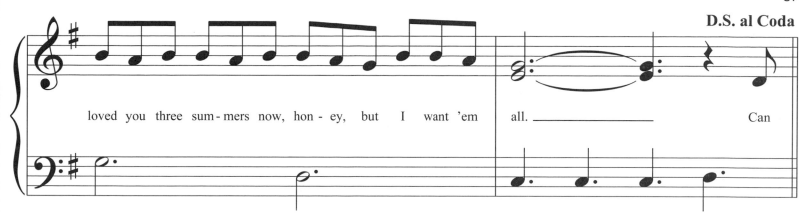

D.S. al Coda

loved you three sum-mers now, hon-ey, but I want 'em all. _____ Can

CODA

La-dies and gen-tle-men, will you please stand? With ev-'ry gui-tar string scar on my hand,

3 I take this mag-net-ic force of a man to be my lov-er. _____ 4

My heart's been bor-rowed and yours has been blue. All's well that ends well, to end up with you.

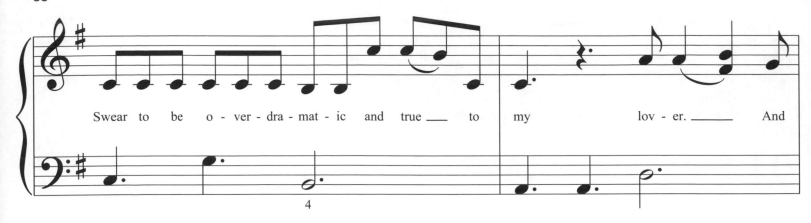

Swear to be o - ver - dra - mat - ic and true ___ to my lov - er. _____ And

you'll save all your dirt - i - est jokes for me. And at ev - 'ry

ta - ble ___ I'll save you a seat, lov - er. _____ Can

I go where you go? _____ Can we al - ways be this

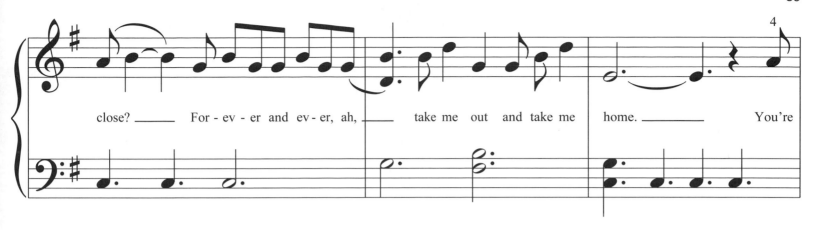

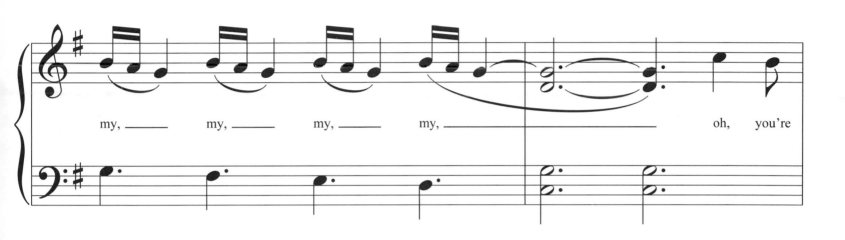

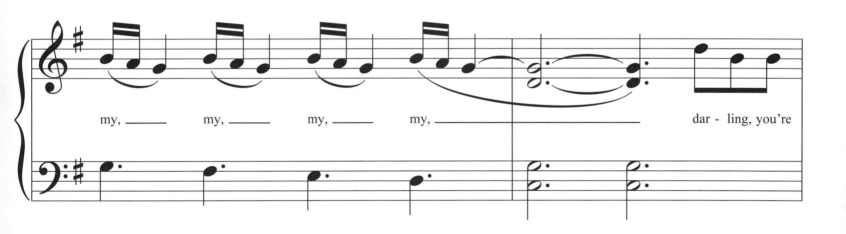

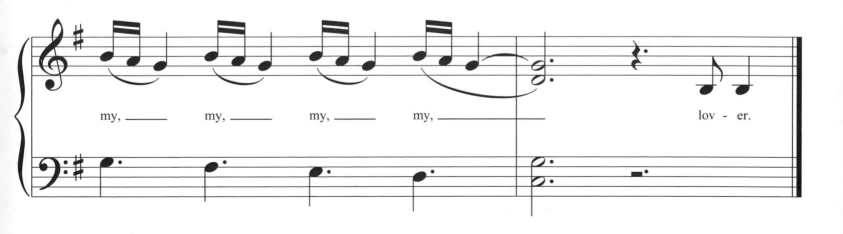

ME!

Words and Music by TAYLOR SWIFT,
JOEL LITTLE and BRENDON URIE

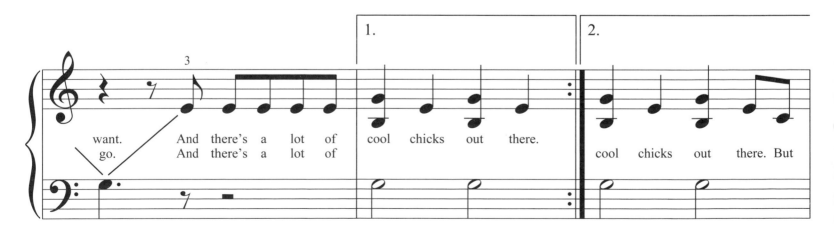

one of these things is not ___ like the oth - ers. Like a rain - bow with all ___

___ of the col - ors. Ba - by doll, when it comes ___ to a lov - er, I

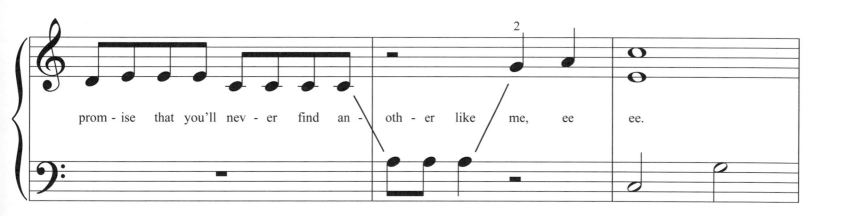

prom - ise that you'll nev - er find an - oth - er like me, ee ee.

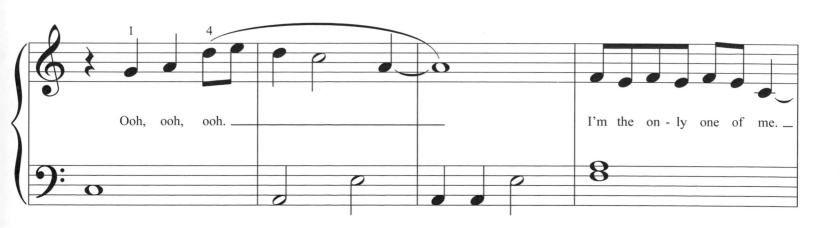

Ooh, ooh, ooh. ___ I'm the on - ly one of me. ___

Ba - by, that's the fun of me, ee ee ee.

Ooh, ooh, ooh.

You're the on - ly one of you. Ba - by, that's the fun of you.

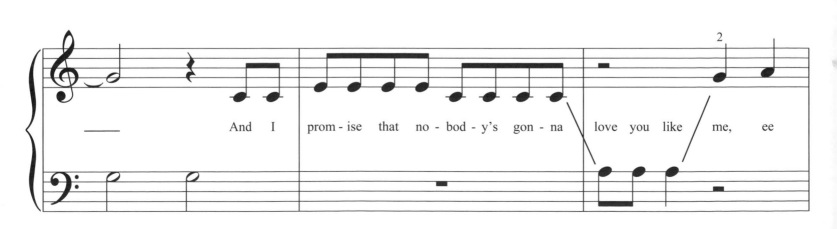

And I prom - ise that no - bod - y's gon - na love you like me, ee

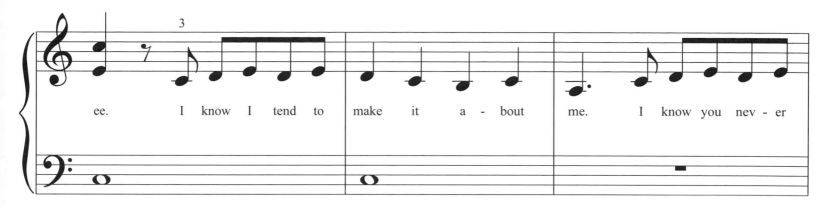

ee.   I know I tend to   make it a - bout   me.   I know you nev - er

get just what you   see.   But I will nev - er   bore you, ba -

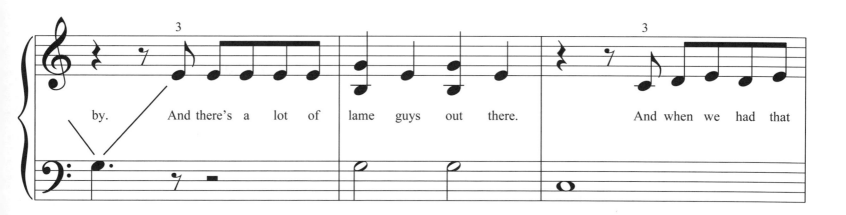

by.   And there's a lot of   lame guys out there.   And when we had that

fight out in the   rain,   you ran af - ter   me and called my

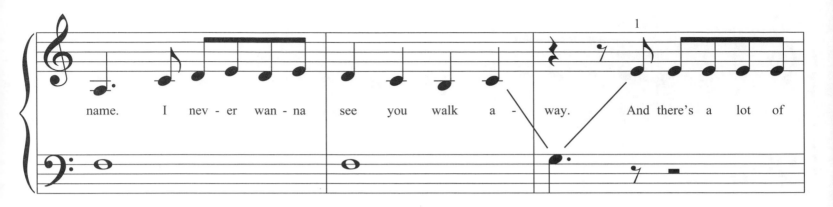

name. I nev - er wan - na see you walk a - way. And there's a lot of

lame guys out there. 'Cause one of these things is not like the oth - ers.

Liv - ing in win - ter, I am your sum - mer. Ba - by doll, when it comes

to a lov - er, I prom - ise that you'll nev - er find an - oth - er like me, ee

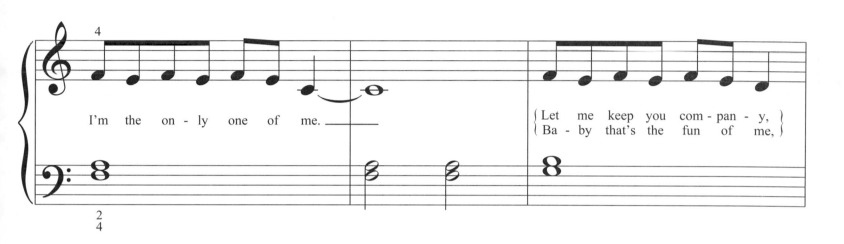

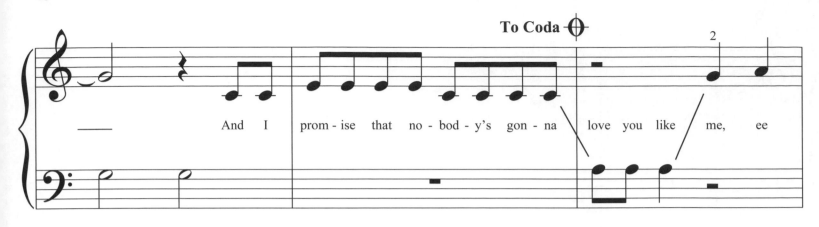

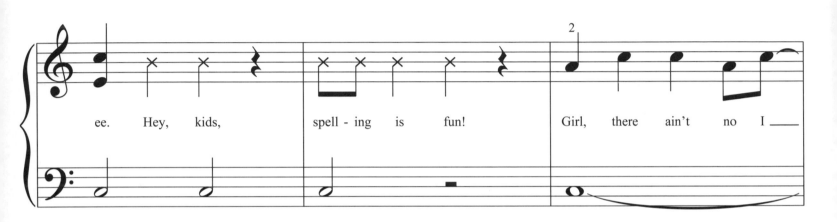

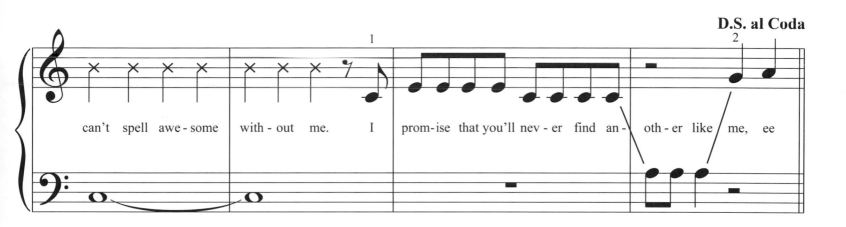

D.S. al Coda

CODA

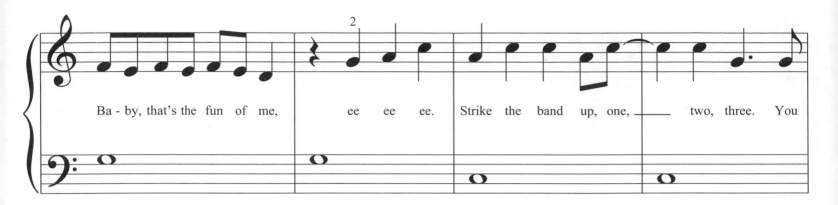

Ba - by, that's the fun of me, ee ee ee. Strike the band up, one, _____ two, three. You

can't spell awe - some with - out me. _____ You're the on - ly one of you. ___

_____ Ba - by, that's the fun of you. ___ _____ And I

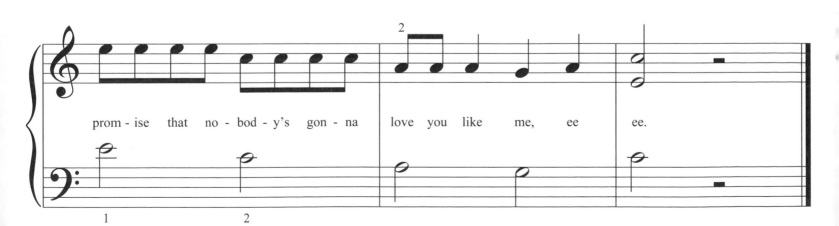

prom - ise that no - bod - y's gon - na love you like me, ee ee.

OUR SONG

Words and Music by
TAYLOR SWIFT

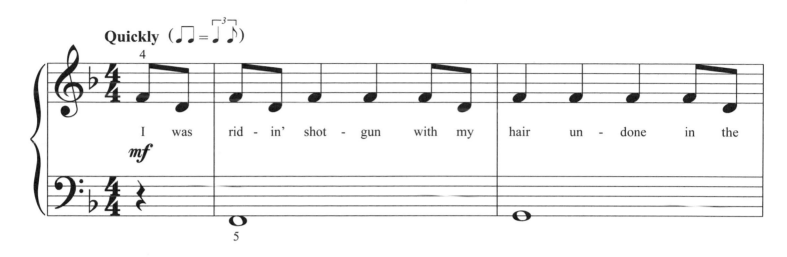

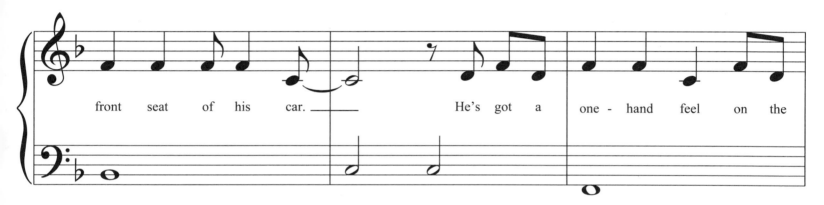

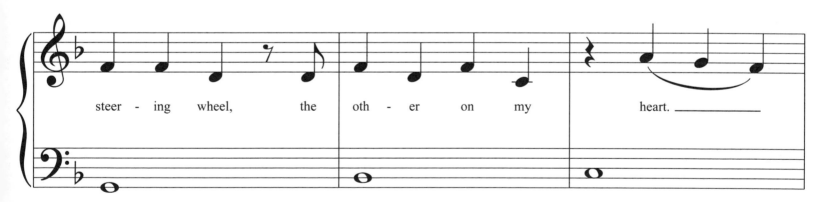

I say, "Noth - in', I was just think - in' how ___

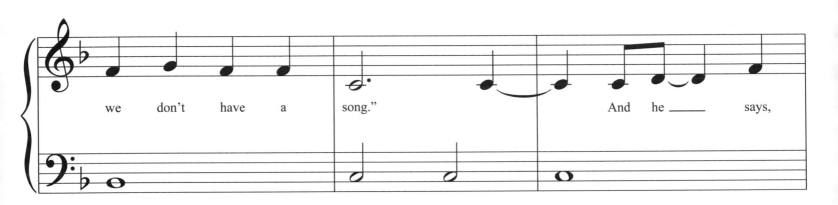

we don't have a song." And he ___ says,

"Our song is a slam - min' screen door, sneak - in' out late, tap - pin'

on your win - dow, when we're on the phone and you talk real ___

slow 'cause it's late and your ma-ma don't know. Our song is the

way you laugh, ___ the first date, 'Man, I did-n't kiss her and I should have.'"

And when I ___ got home, 'fore I

To Coda ⊕

said, ___ "A - men," ask - in' God ___ if He ___ could

play it a - gain.

I was walk - in' up the

front porch steps af - ter ev - 'ry - thing that day ___ had

gone all wrong, ___ had been tram - pled on ___ and a - lost and thrown a -

way. _____ Got to the hall - way, well on my way

to my lov - in' bed. _____ I al - most did - n't no - tice

D.S. al Coda

all the ros - es and the note that said, _____

CODA

play it a - gain. _____ Da, da, da, da. _____ I've

heard   ev - 'ry   al - bum,   lis - tened   to   the   ra - di -

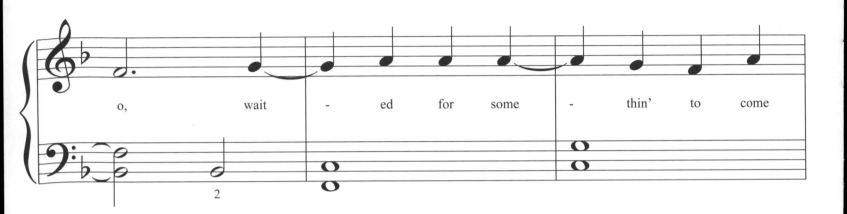

o,   wait - ed   for   some - thin'   to   come

a - long _____   that was as   good as our ___ song. ___

___   'Cause our   song   is a   slam - min' screen door,

sneak - in' out late, tap - pin' on his win - dow, when we're on the phone —

— and he talks real slow 'cause it's late and his ma - ma don't

know. Our song is the way he laughs, — the first date, "Man, I did - n't

kiss him and I should have." And when I ___ got

home,   'fore I   said, _____ "A -   men,"   ask - in'

God _____ if   he _____   could   play   it   a - gain. _____

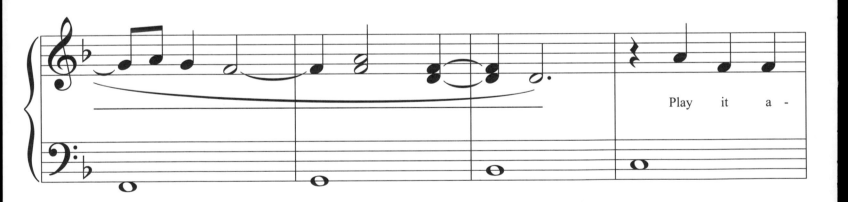

Play   it   a -

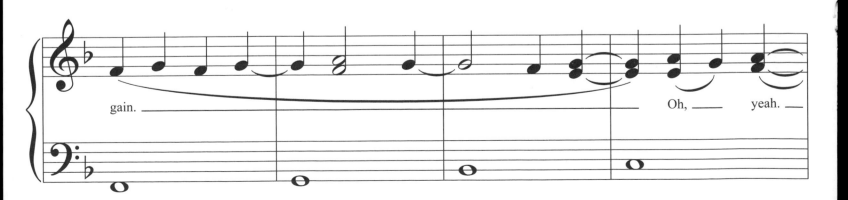

gain. _____   Oh, _____ yeah. _____

Oh, _____ oh, _____ yeah.

I was rid - in' shot - gun with my hair un - done in the

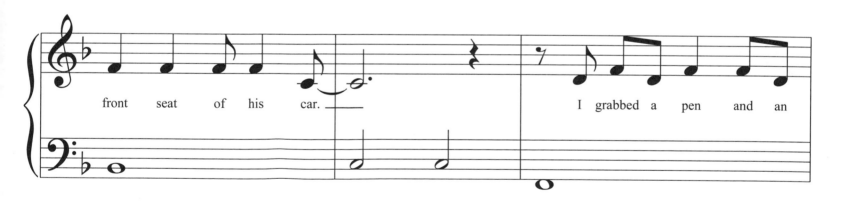

front seat of his car. _____ I grabbed a pen and an

old nap - kin and I wrote down our _____ song.

rit.

MEAN

Words and Mu
TAYLOR SW.

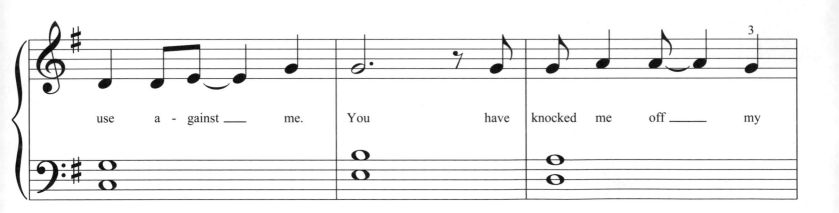

voice like nails on a chalk-board call-ing me out _____ when I'm wound-ed.

You, pick-ing on the weak-er man. _____

Well, you can take me down _____

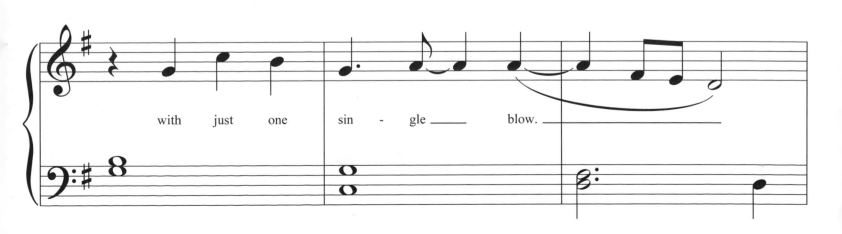

with just one sin - gle ____ blow. ____

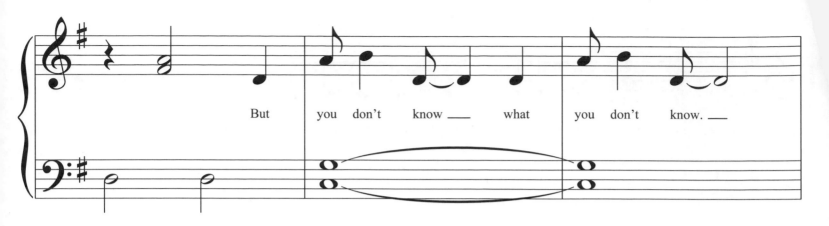

But you don't know ___ what you don't know. ___

Some - day ___ I'll be ___ liv - ing in a big ole

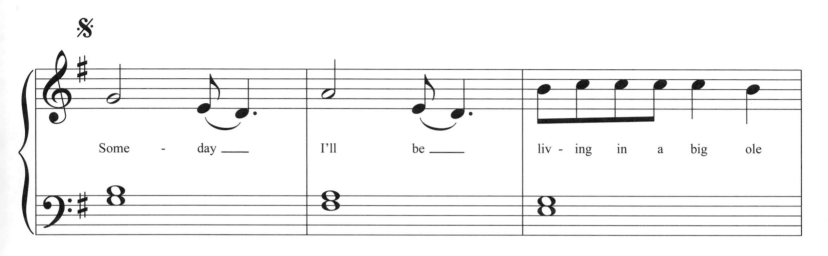

cit - y, ___ and all you're ___ ev - er gon - na be is

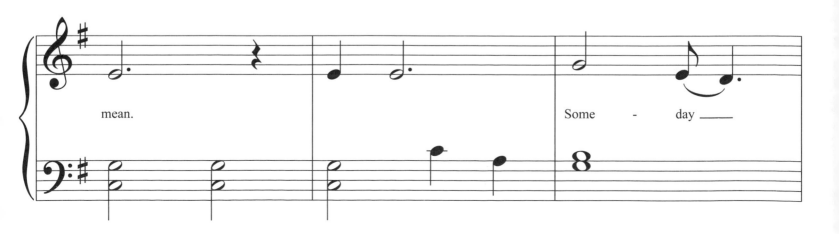

mean. Some - day ___

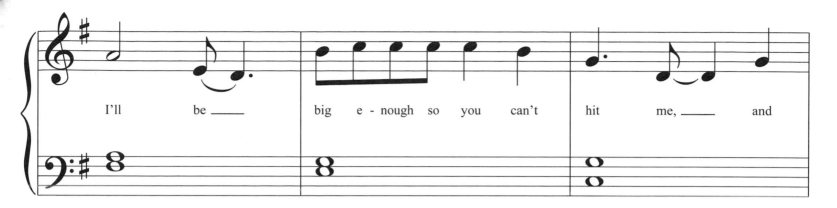

I'll be _____ big e - nough so you can't hit me, _____ and

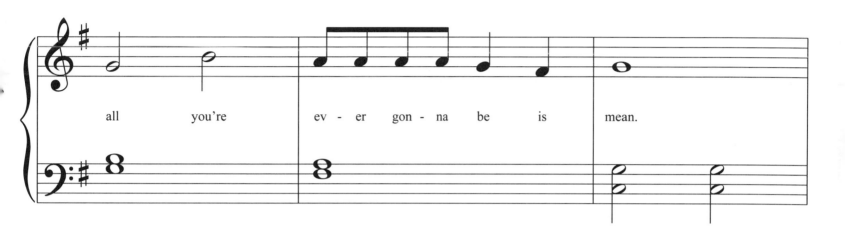

all you're ev - er gon - na be is mean.

To Coda ⊕

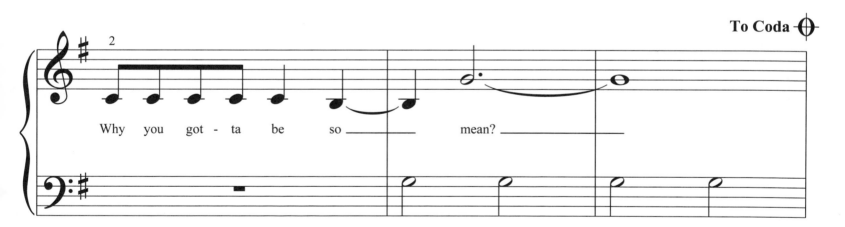

Why you got - ta be so _____ mean? _____

You, with your

switch - ing sides and your wild - fire lies and your hu - mil - i - a - tion.

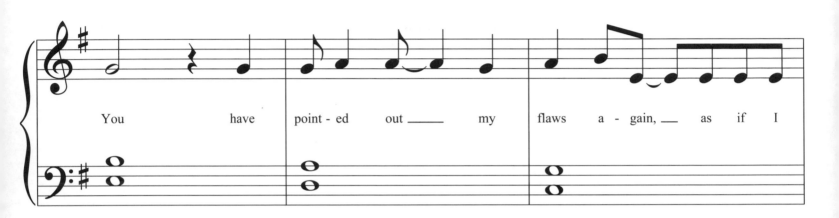

You have point - ed out ____ my flaws a - gain, ___ as if I

don't al - read - y see them. I walk with my head down, ___ try'n' to

block you out 'cause I'll nev - er im - press you. I just

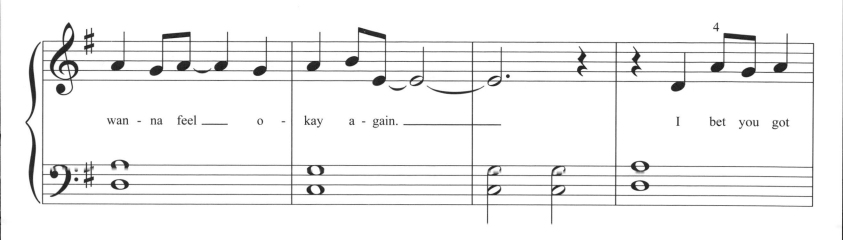

wan - na feel ____ o - kay a - gain. ____ I bet you got

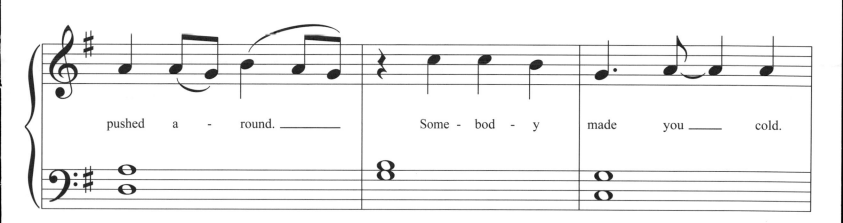

pushed a - round. _____ Some - bod - y made you ____ cold.

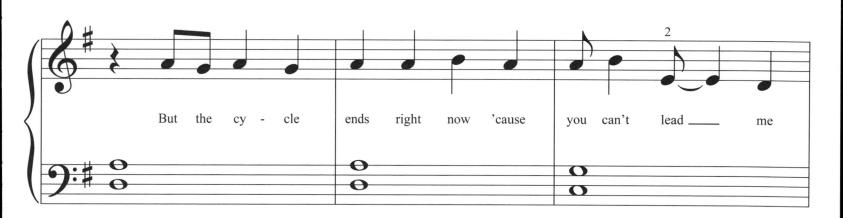

But the cy - cle ends right now 'cause you can't lead ____ me

D.S. al Coda

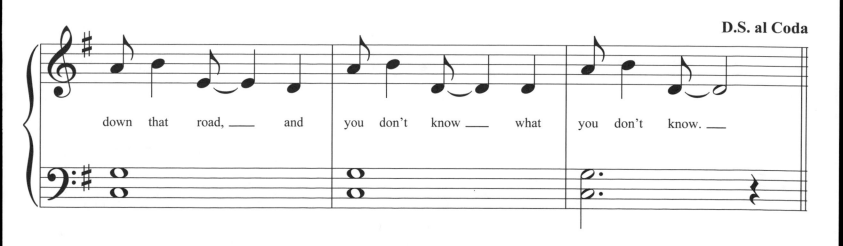

down that road, ____ and you don't know ____ what you don't know. ____

CODA

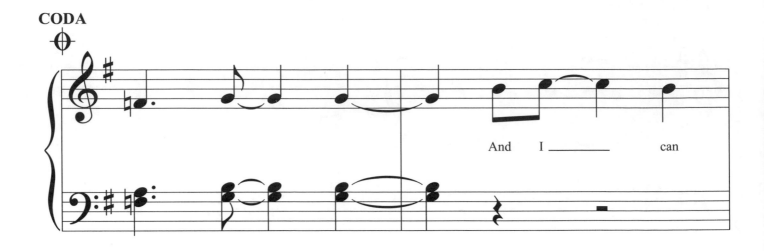

And I _____ can

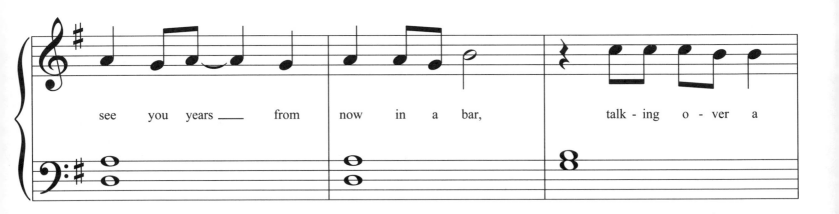

see you years ____ from now in a bar, talk - ing o - ver a

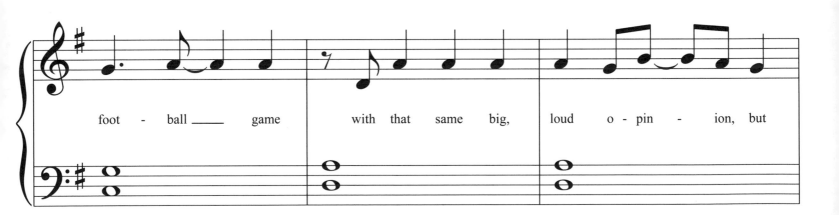

foot - ball ____ game with that same big, loud o - pin - ion, but

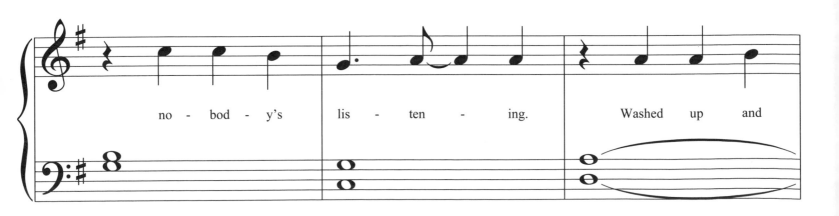

no - bod - y's lis - ten - ing. Washed up and

rant - ing a - bout the same old

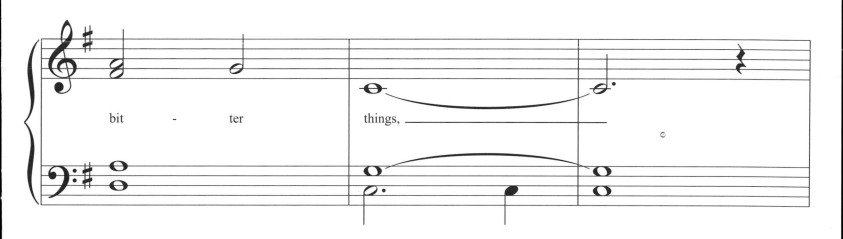

bit - ter things,

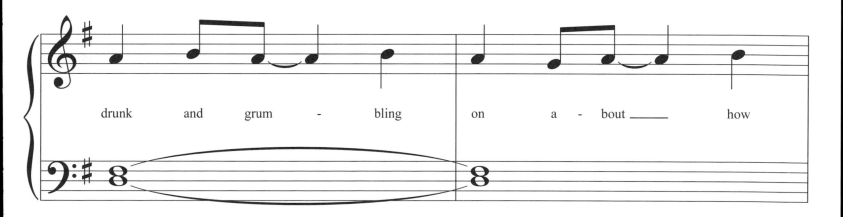

drunk and grum - bling on a - bout _____ how

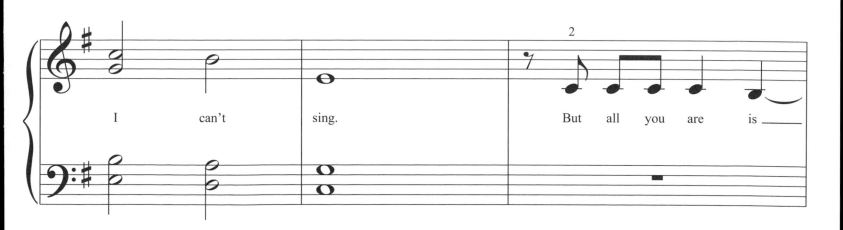

I can't sing. But all you are is _____

65

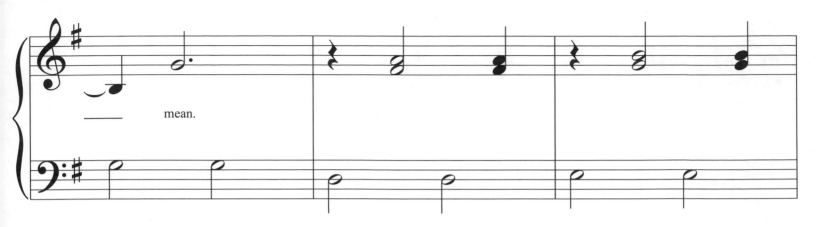

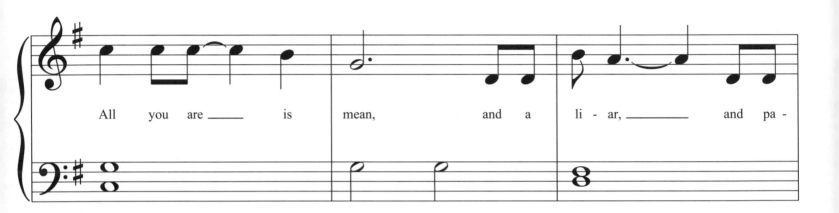

mean.

All you are _____ is mean, and a li - ar, _____ and pa -

thet - ic, _____ and a - lone in life, _____ and mean and

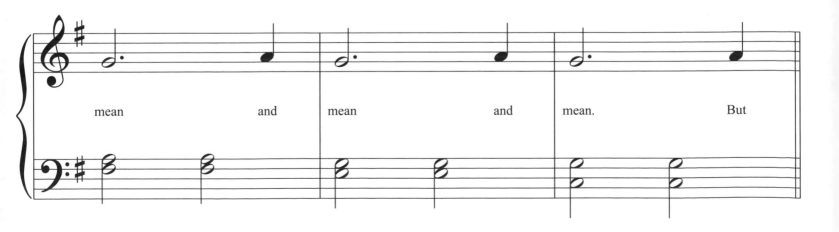

mean and mean and mean. But

some - day ____ I'll be ____ liv - ing in a big ole
some - day ____ I'll be ____ big e - nough so you can't

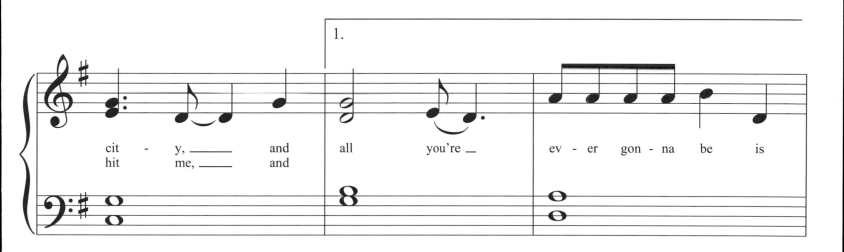

1.

cit - y, ____ and all you're ____ ev - er gon - na be is
hit me, ____ and

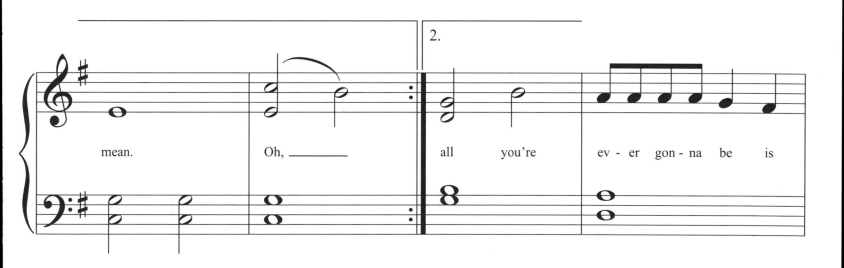

2.

mean. Oh, ____ all you're ev - er gon - na be is

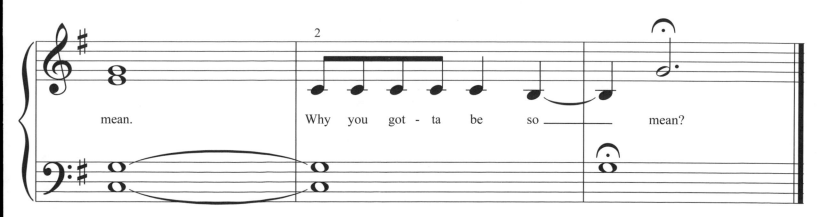

2

mean. Why you got - ta be so ____ mean?

MINE

Words and Music by
TAYLOR SWIFT

left a small ___ town,   nev - er looked back. ___   I was a flight ___ risk
And there's a drawer ___ of   my things at   your place.   You learn my se - crets and you fig -

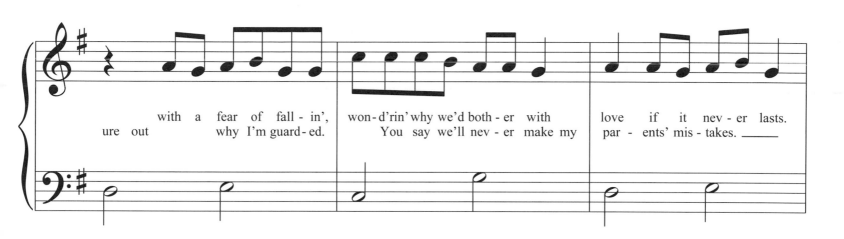

with a fear of fall - in',   won - d'rin' why we'd both - er with   love if it nev - er lasts.
ure out   why I'm guard - ed.   You say we'll nev - er make my   par - ents' mis - takes. _____

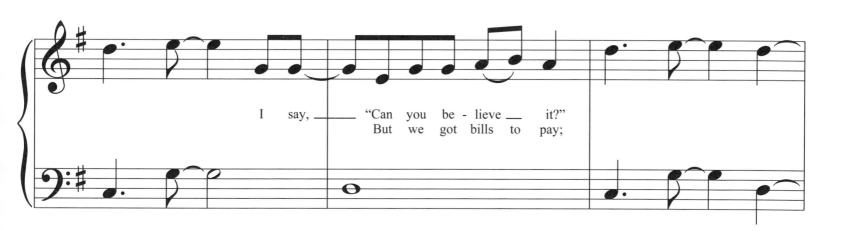

I say, _____ "Can you be - lieve ___ it?"
But we got bills to pay;

as we're ly - in' on the   couch,   the mo - ment I could see ___ it.
we got noth - in' fig - ured   out.   When it was hard to take,

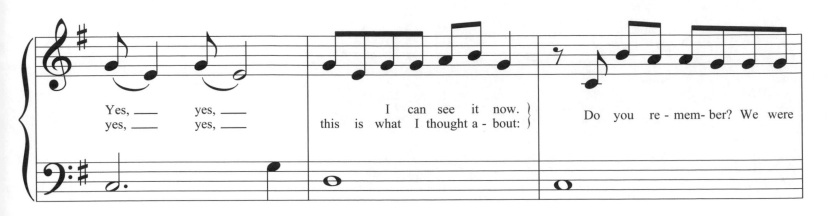

Yes, ___ yes, ___ I can see it now.
yes, ___ yes, ___ this is what I thought a - bout:
Do you re - mem- ber? We were

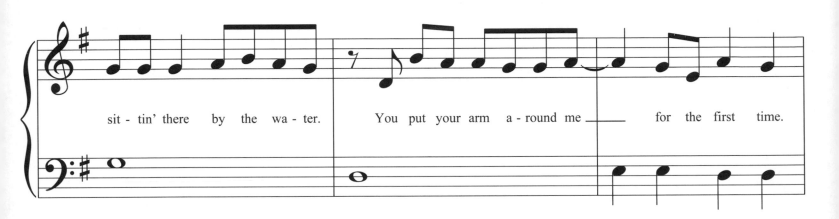

sit - tin' there by the wa - ter.
You put your arm a - round me ___ for the first time.

You made a reb - el of a care - less man's care - ful daugh- ter.
You are the best thing

1.

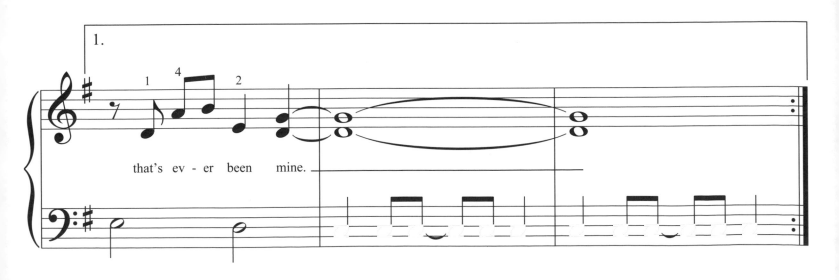

that's ev - er been mine. ___

Oh, oh, ___ oh. ___

And I re - mem - ber that fight, two - thir - ty A. M., 'cause

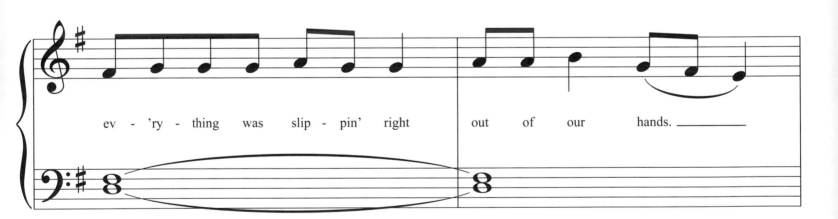

ev - 'ry - thing was slip - pin' right out of our hands. ___

I ran out cry - in' and you fol - lowed me out in - to the street.

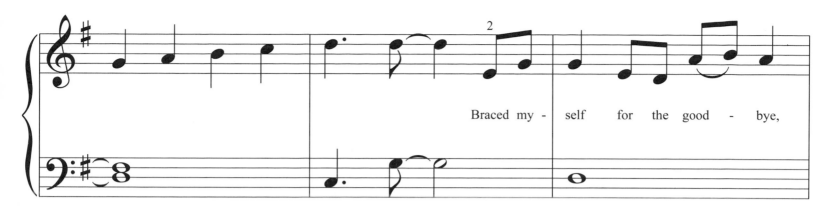

Braced my - self for the good - bye,

'cause that's all I've ev - er known. ___ And you

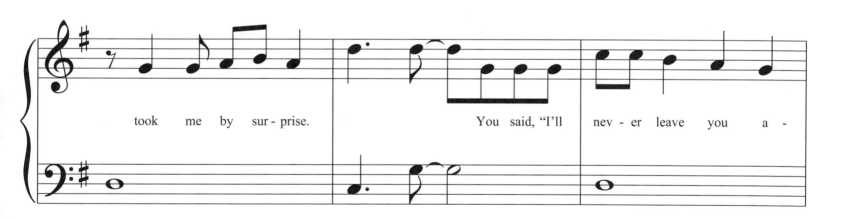

took me by sur - prise. You said, "I'll nev - er leave you a -

lone." ___ You said, "I re - mem - ber how we

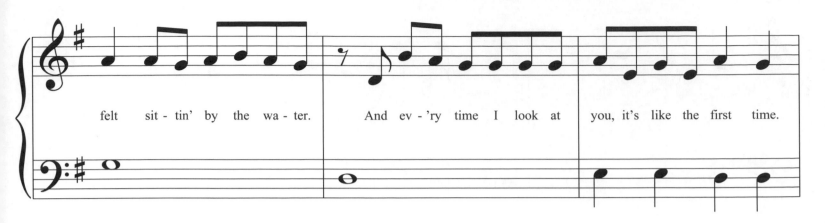

felt sit - tin' by the wa - ter. And ev - 'ry time I look at you, it's like the first time.

I fell in love with a care - less man's care - ful daugh - ter. She is the best ___ thing

that's ev - er been ___ mine." (Hold ___ on, ___ and

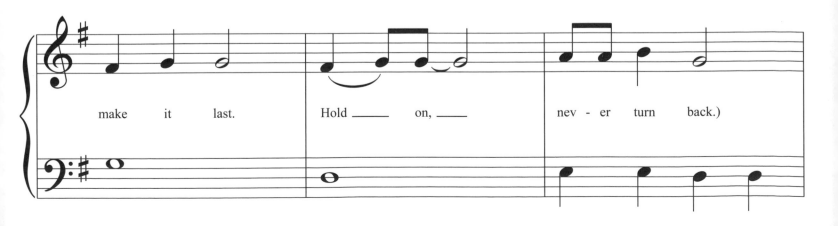

make it last. Hold ___ on, ___ nev - er turn back.)

You made a reb-el of a care-less man's care-ful daugh-ter. You are the best thing

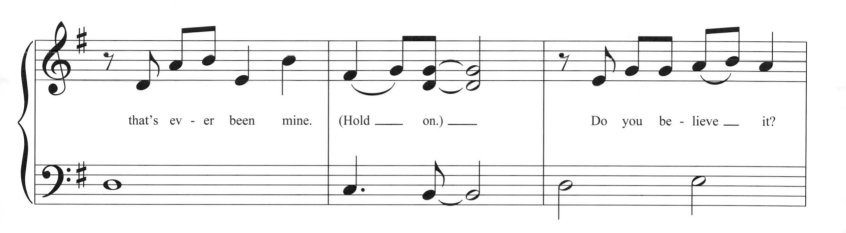

that's ev-er been mine. (Hold ___ on.) ___ Do you be-lieve ___ it?

(Hold ___ on.) ___ We're gon-na make it now. (Hold ___ on.) ___

And I can see ___ it.

PICTURE TO BURN

Words and Music by TAYLOR SWIFT
and LIZ ROSE

that I'm ob - ses - sive and cra - zy. That's fine, you won't __ mind if I

say, by the way, I hate that stu - pid old pick - up truck you

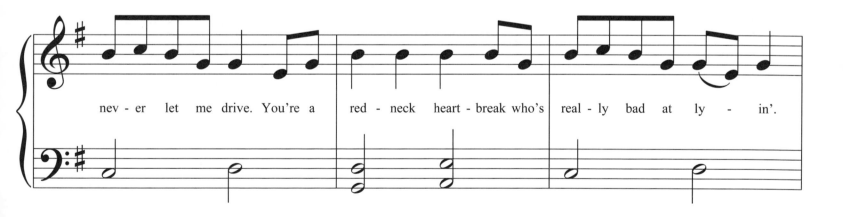

nev - er let me drive. You're a red - neck heart - break who's real - ly bad at ly - in'.

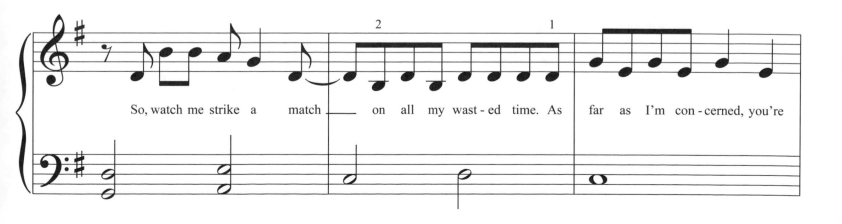

So, watch me strike a match __ on all my wast - ed time. As far as I'm con - cerned, you're

just an-oth-er pic-ture to burn.

There's no time for tears, I'm just sit-tin' here plan-nin' my re-

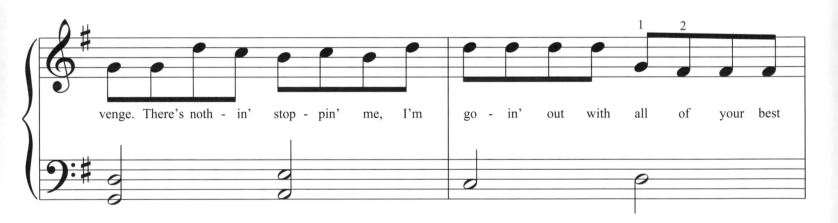

venge. There's noth-in' stop-pin' me, I'm go-in' out with all of your best

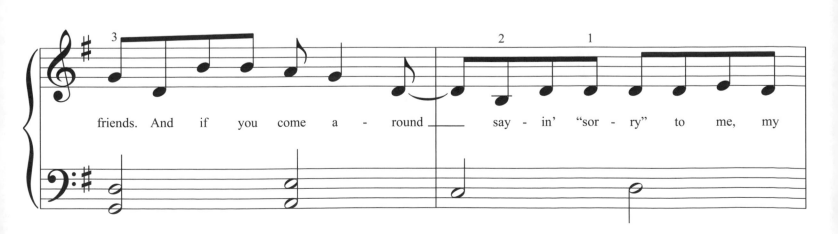

friends. And if you come a - round say-in' "sor-ry" to me, my

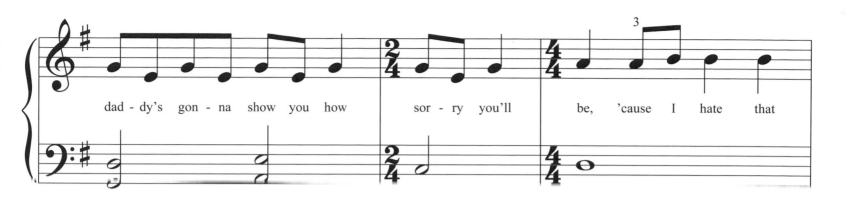

dad - dy's gon - na show you how sor - ry you'll be, 'cause I hate that

stu - pid old pick - up truck you nev - er let me drive. You're a red - neck heart - break who's

real - ly bad at ly - in'. So, watch me strike a match on all my was - ted time. As

far as I'm con - cerned, you're just an - oth - er pic - ture to burn.

And

if you're miss-in' me, you bet-ter keep it to your-self, 'cause com-in' back a-round here would be

bad for your health, _____ 'cause I hate that stu-pid old pick-up truck you

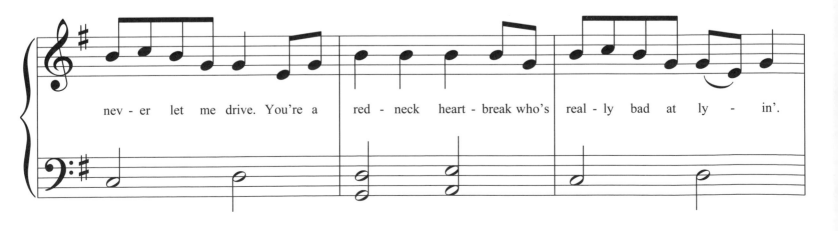

nev-er let me drive. You're a red-neck heart-break who's real-ly bad at ly - in'.

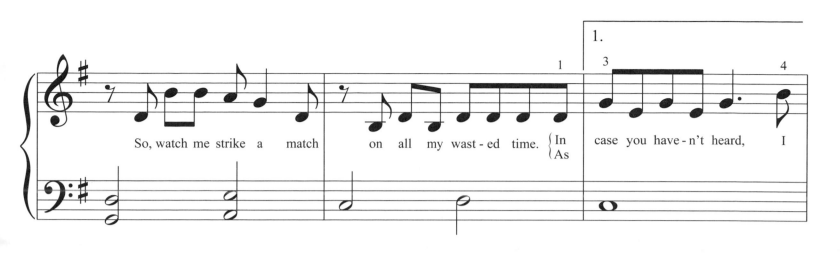

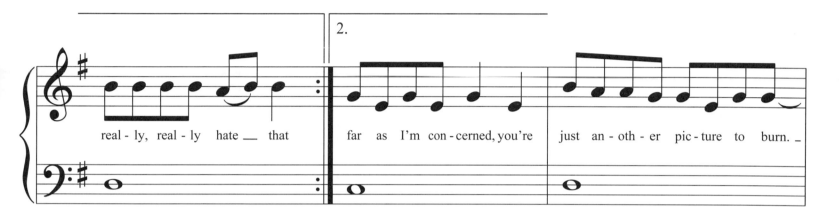

SHAKE IT OFF

Words and Music by TAYLOR SWIFT,
MAX MARTIN and SHELLBACK

at least, that's what peo - ple say, _____ mm, mm. That's what peo - ple
And that's what they don't know, _____ mm, mm. That's what they don't

say, _____ mm, mm. But I keep cruis - ing;
know, _____ mm, mm. But I keep cruis - ing;

can't stop, won't stop mov - ing. } It's like I got this
can't stop, won't stop groov - ing. }

mu - sic in my mind say - ing, "It's gon - na be al -

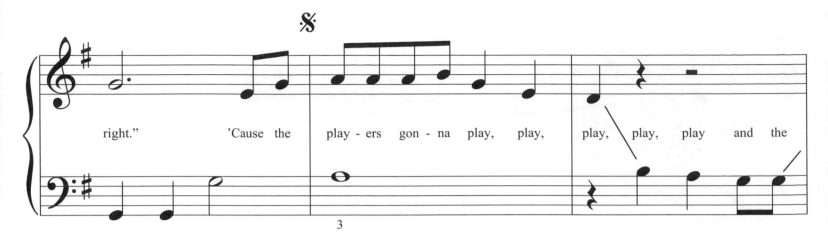

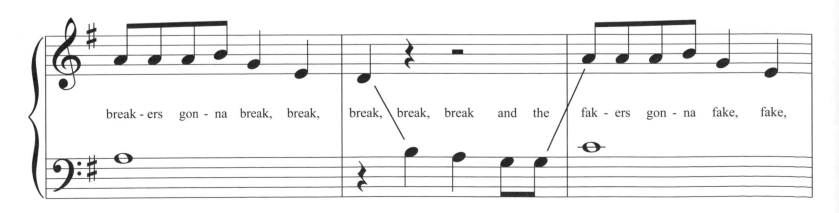

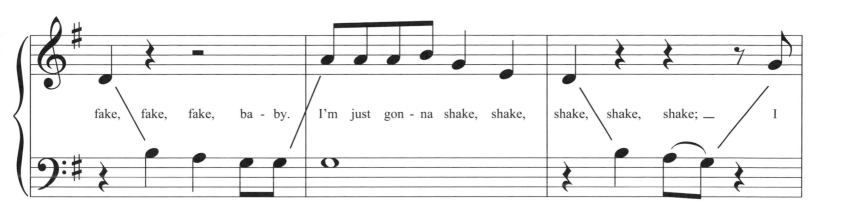

fake, fake, fake, ba-by. I'm just gon-na shake, shake, shake, shake, shake; ___ I

To Coda

1. 2.

shake it off, I shake it off. I nev-er miss a off. I

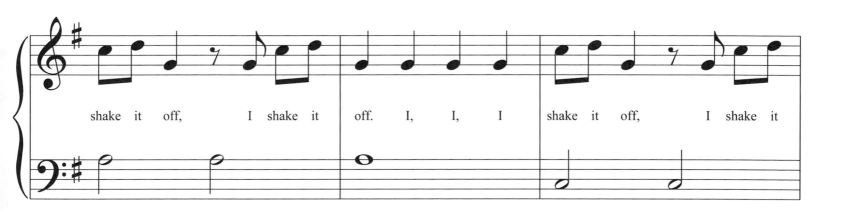

shake it off, I shake it off. I, I, I shake it off, I shake it

off. I, I, I shake it off, I shake it off. I, I, I

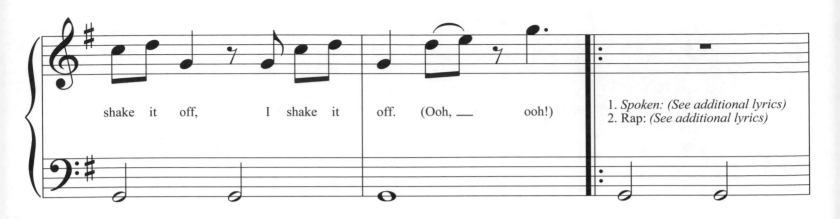

shake it off,   I shake it   off.   (Ooh, __ ooh!)

1. *Spoken: (See additional lyrics)*
2. Rap: *(See additional lyrics)*

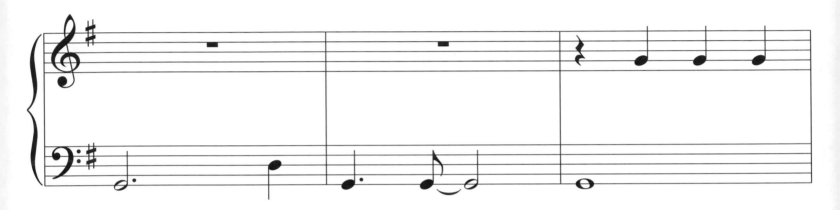

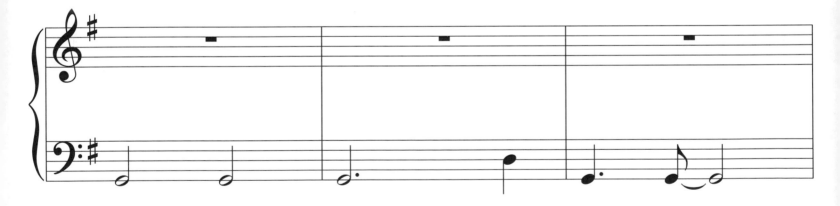

D.S. al Coda

Rap ends   Yeah,   oh. _____ 'Cause the

CODA

off. (Ooh, ___ ooh!) I shake it off, I shake it off. I, I, I

shake it off, I shake it off. I, I, I shake it off, I shake it off. I, I, I

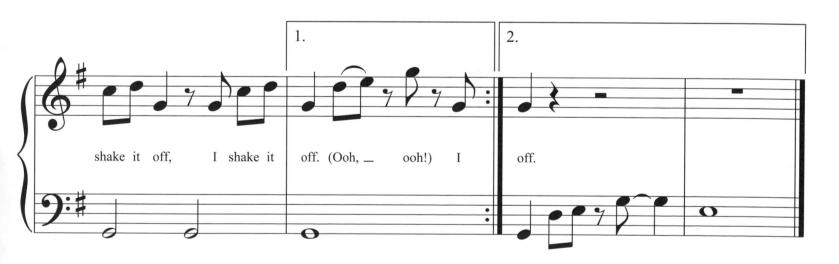

1.
shake it off, I shake it off. (Ooh, ___ ooh!) I

2.
off.

Additional Lyrics

Spoken: Hey, hey, hey! Just think: While you've been getting
Down and out about the liars and the dirty, dirty
Cheats of the world, you could've been getting down to
This. Sick. Beat!

Rap: My ex-man brought his new girlfriend.
She's like, "Oh, my God!" But I'm just gonna shake.
And to the fella over there with the hella good hair,
Won't you come on over, baby? We can shake, shake, shake.

WE ARE NEVER EVER GETTING BACK TOGETHER

Words and Music by TAYLOR SWIFT,
SHELLBACK and MAX MARTIN

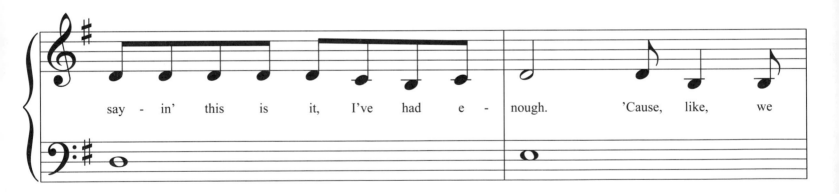

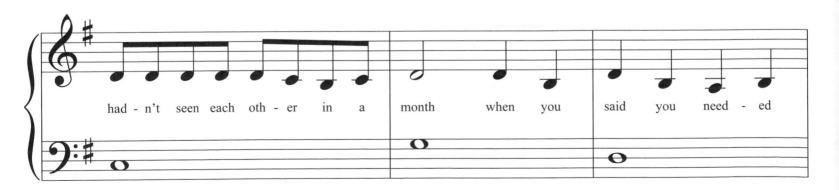

space. What? Then you come a-round a-gain and say, "Ba - by, I
real - ly gon - na miss you pick - ing fights, and me

miss you and I swear I'm gon - na change. Trust me." Re -
fall - ing for it, scream - ing that I'm right. And you would

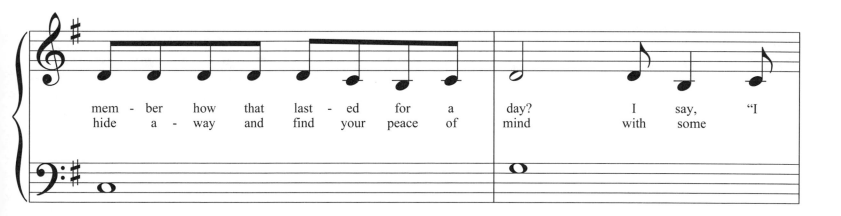

mem - ber how that last - ed for a day? I say, "I
hide a - way and find your peace of mind with some

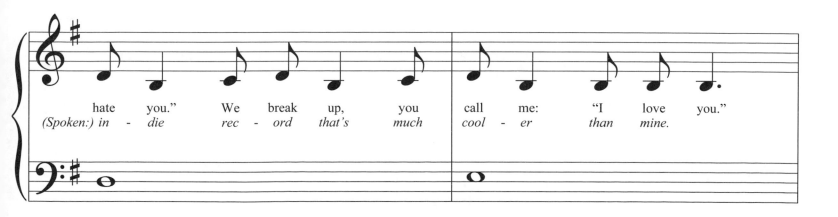

hate you." We break up, you call me: "I love you."
(Spoken:) in - die rec - ord that's much cool - er than mine.

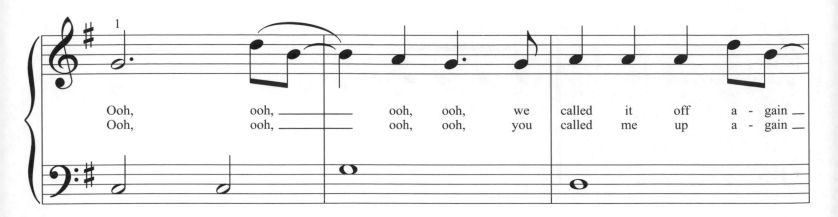

Ooh, ooh, _____ ooh, ooh, we called it off a - gain _____
Ooh, ooh, _____ ooh, ooh, you called me up a - gain _____

_____ last night.
_____ to - night. } But ooh, ooh, _____ ooh, ooh, this time I'm

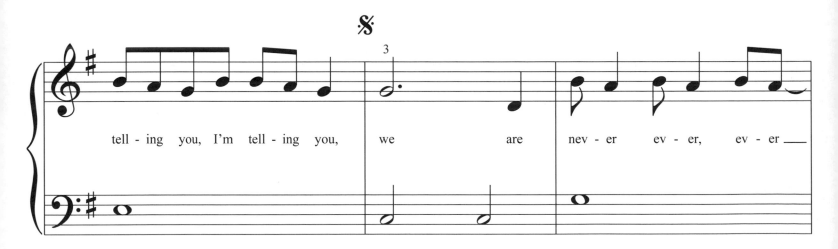

tell - ing you, I'm tell - ing you, we are nev - er ev - er, ev - er _____

_____ get - ting back to - geth - er. We _____ are nev - er ev - er, ev - er _____

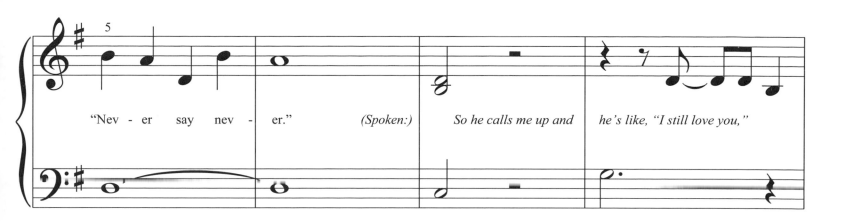

"Nev - er say nev - er." *(Spoken:)* *So he calls me up and* *he's like, "I still love you,"*

and I'm like... I'm just... *I mean, this is exhausting, you know?*

D.S. al Coda

Like, we are never getting back *together,* *like,* *ev - er.* *No,*

CODA

get - ting back. ___ We, ooh, ___ ooh, ooh,

STYLE

Words and Music by TAYLOR SWIFT,
MAX MARTIN, SHELLBACK
and ALI PAYAMI

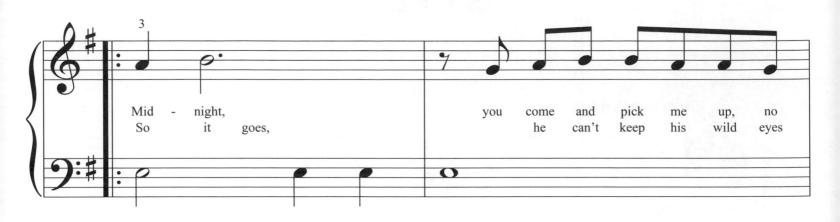

Mid - night, you come and pick me up, no
So it goes, he can't keep his wild eyes

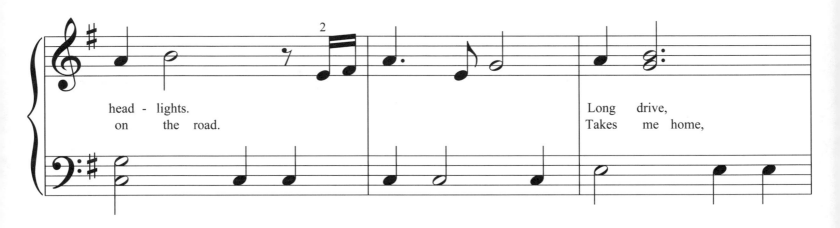

head - lights. Long drive,
on the road. Takes me home,

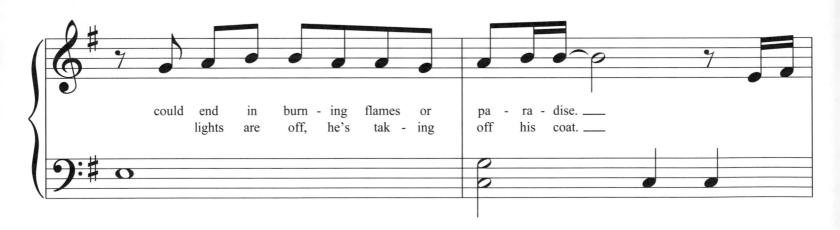

could end in burn - ing flames or pa - ra - dise. ___
lights are off, he's tak - ing off his coat. ___

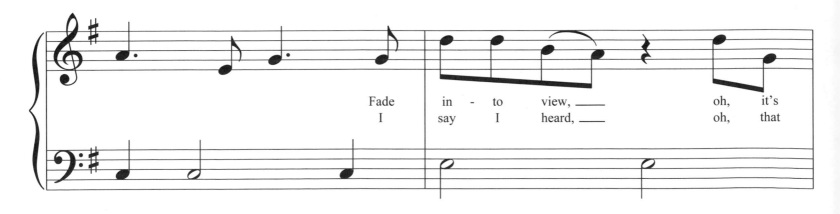

Fade in - to view, ___ oh, it's
I say I heard, ___ oh, that

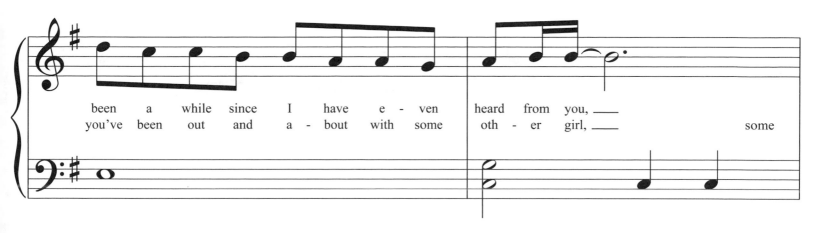

been a while since I have e - ven heard from you, ____ some

you've been out and a - bout with some oth - er girl, ____

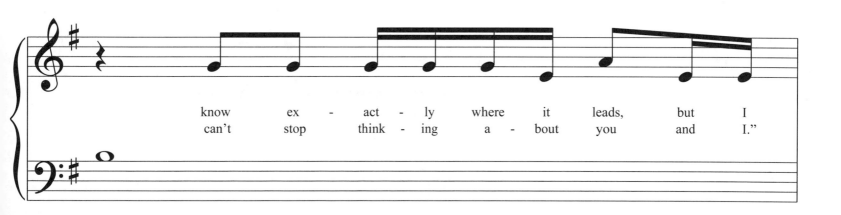

heard from you. ____ And I should just tell you to leave 'cause I

oth - er girl. ____ He says, "What you've heard is true, but I

know ex - act - ly where it leads, but I

can't stop think - ing a - bout you and I."

watch us go round and round each time. ____ You got that

I said, "I've been there too, a few times." You got that

James Dean day - dream look in your eye _____ and I got that

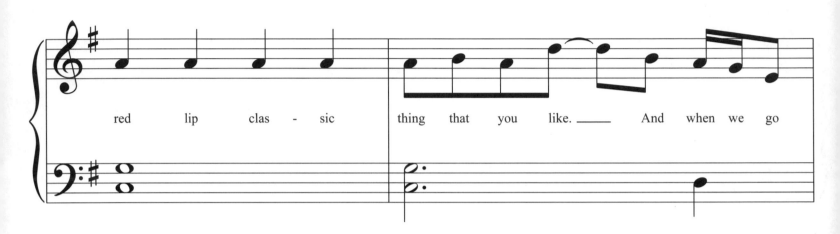

red lip clas - sic thing that you like. _____ And when we go

crash - ing down, we come back ev - 'ry time _____ 'cause we nev - er go

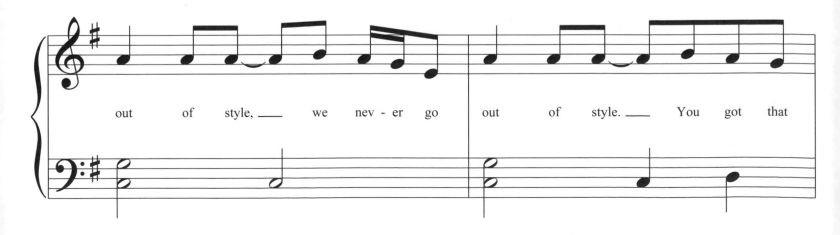

out of style, _____ we nev - er go out of style. _____ You got that

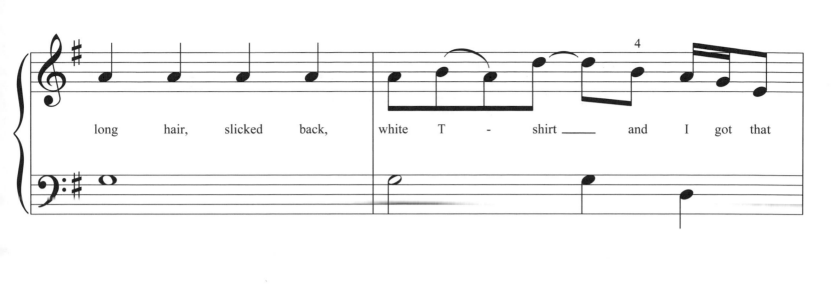

long hair, slicked back, white T - shirt ____ and I got that

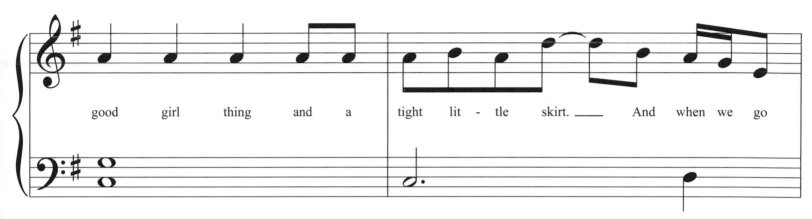

good girl thing and a tight lit - tle skirt. ____ And when we go

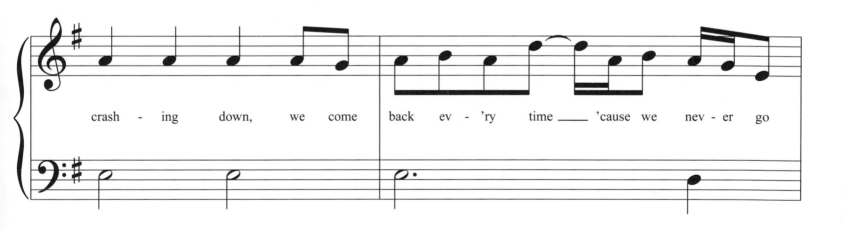

crash - ing down, we come back ev - 'ry time ____ 'cause we nev - er go

out of style, ____ we nev - er go out of style. ____

James __ Dean day - dream look in your eye __ and I got that

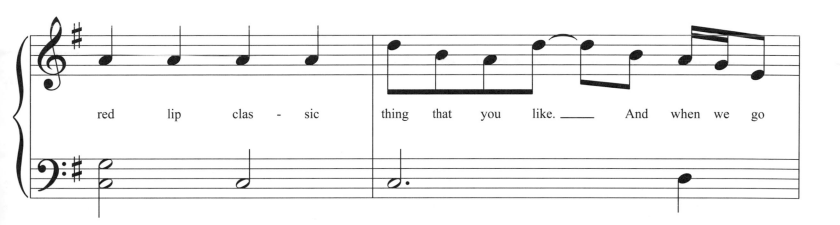

red lip clas - sic thing that you like. __ And when we go

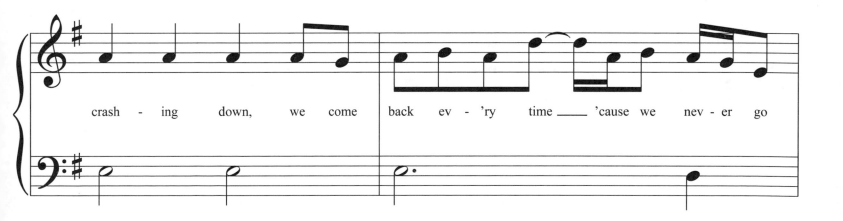

crash - ing down, we come back ev - 'ry time __ 'cause we nev - er go

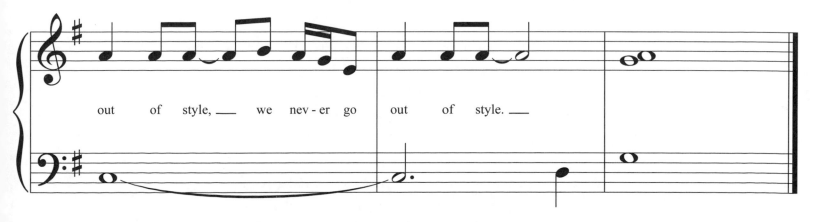

out of style, __ we nev - er go out of style. __

22

Words and Music by TAYLOR SWIFT,
SHELLBACK and MAX MARTIN

Moderately fast

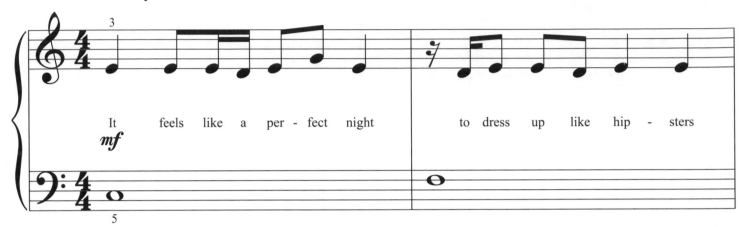

Uh, uh, uh, uh. Yeah, _____ we're

hap - py, free, con - fused and lone - ly {at the same time.} {in the best way.} It's

mis - 'ra - ble and mag - i - cal. Oh, _____ yeah, _____ to -

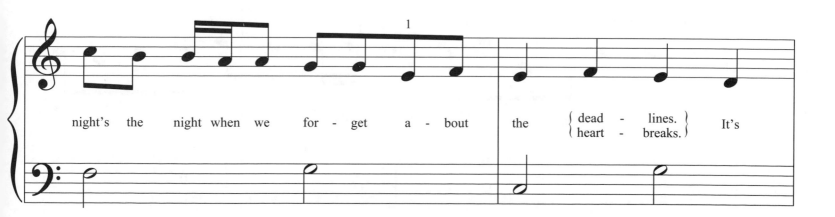

night's the night when we for - get a - bout the {dead - lines.} {heart - breaks.} It's

time. Oh, oh. I don't know a-bout you,

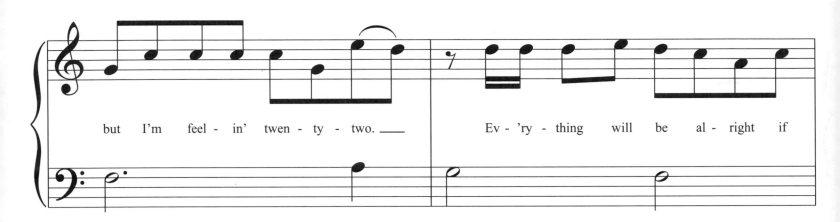

but I'm feel-in' twen-ty-two. ___ Ev-'ry-thing will be al-right if

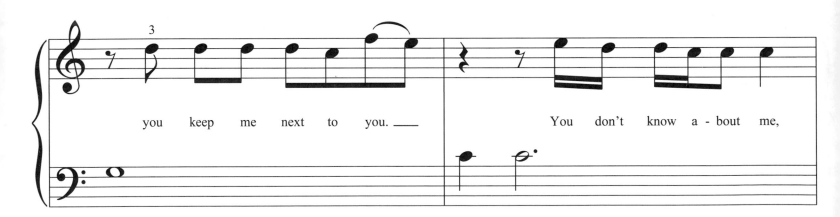

you keep me next to you. ___ You don't know a-bout me,

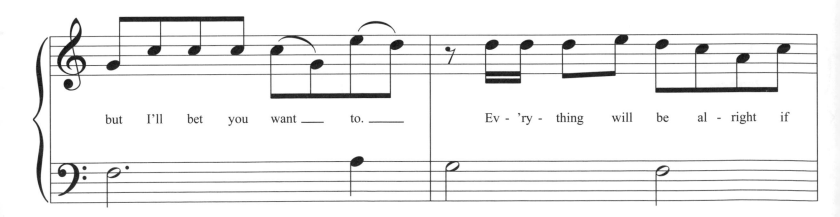

but I'll bet you want ___ to. ___ Ev-'ry-thing will be al-right if

we just keep danc - in' like we're twen - ty - two. ____

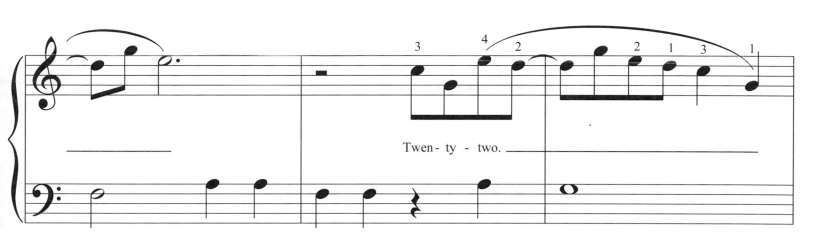

____ Twen - ty - two. _____

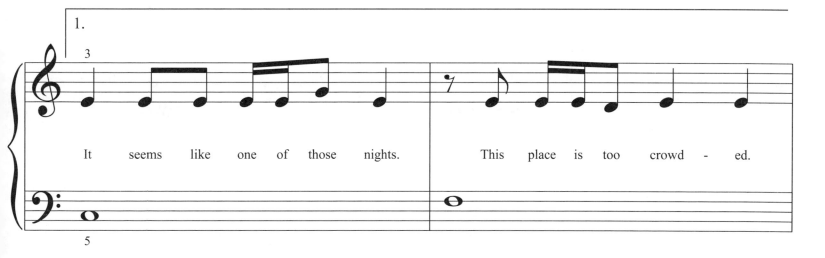

1.

It seems like one of those nights. This place is too crowd - ed.

5

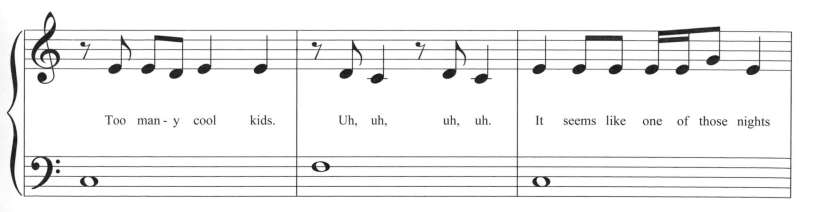

Too man - y cool kids. Uh, uh, uh, uh. It seems like one of those nights

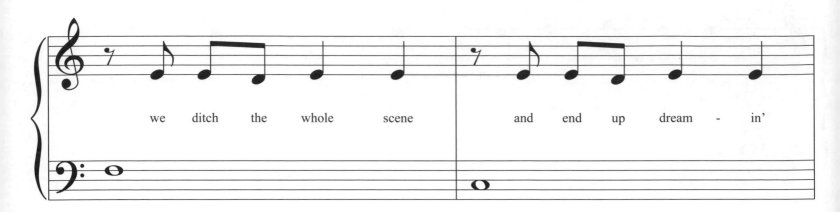

we ditch the whole scene and end up dream - in'

in - stead of sleep - in'. Twen - ty - two.

Twen - ty - two. It feels like one of those nights

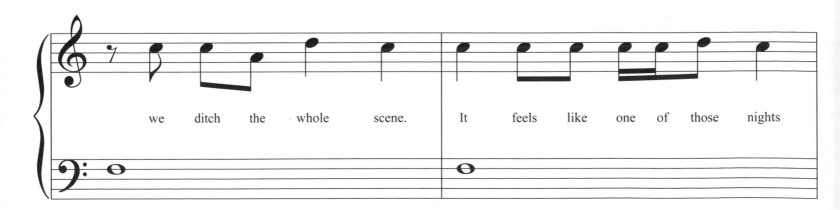

we ditch the whole scene. It feels like one of those nights

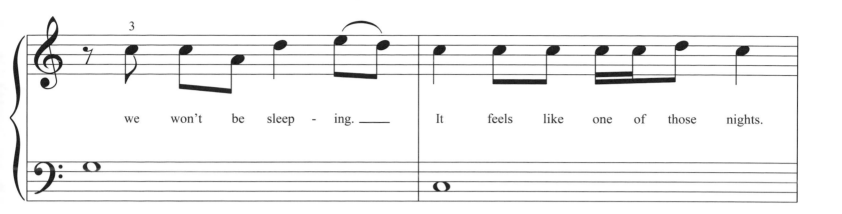

we won't be sleep - ing.____ It feels like one of those nights.

To Coda ✛

You look like bad news. I got - ta have you.

I got - ta have you.____ Oo, ____

D.S. al Coda
(take 2nd ending)

CODA
✛

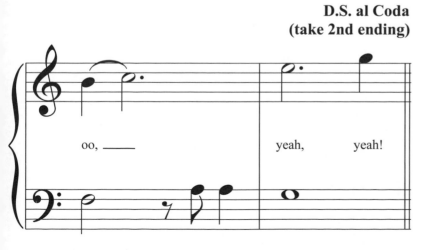

oo, ____ yeah, yeah!

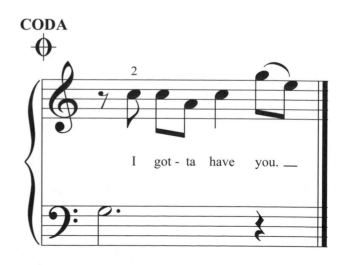

I got - ta have you. __

YOU NEED TO CALM DOWN

Words and Music by TAYLOR SWIFT
and JOEL LITTLE

say it in a tweet, that's a cop- out. And I'm just like,
you would rath- er be in the dark ag - es. Mak-ing that

"Hey, ___ are you o -
sign ___ must have tak- en all

kay?" ___ And
night. ___

I ain't try'n' to mess with your self - ex - pres-sion but I've learned the les-
You just need to take sev -'ral seats and then try to re - store the peace

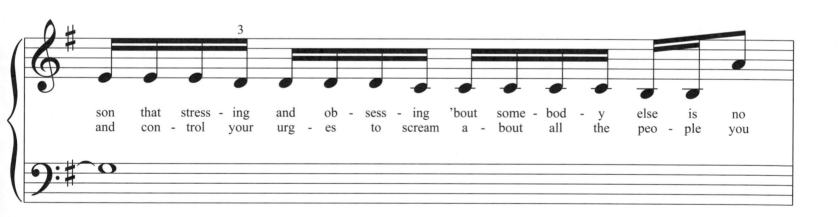

son that stress - ing and ob- sess - ing 'bout some- bod - y else is no
and con - trol your urg - es to scream a - bout all the peo - ple you

fun.
hate;

And snakes and stones nev - er broke my bones.}
'cause shade nev - er made an - y - bod - y less gay.} So

2

oh, oh, (Oh, oh, oh, oh, oh, oh, oh, oh.) _____ you need to calm

down. _____ You're be - ing too loud. _____ And I'm just like,

oh, oh, (Oh, oh, oh, oh, oh, oh, oh, oh.) _____ you need to just

stop. _____ Like, can you just not _____ step on {my}{his} gown? You need to calm

oh, oh.) ____ You need to calm down. ____ You're be - ing too

loud. ____ And I'm just like, oh, oh, (Oh, oh, oh, oh, oh, oh,

oh, oh.) ____ you need to just stop. ____ Like, can you just

not ____ step on our gowns? You need to calm down.